Tips, Techniques and Tools To Master The Hunt

The Job Hunting Tool Kit I - IV

Tips, Techniques and Tools

to Master Your Job Hunt

By George Valentine

www.jobhunterstoolkit.com

Tips, Techniques and Tools To Master The Hunt

Table of Contents:

Sec tion I Building On The Basics….. 3

First steps forming the foundation of a winning job hunt. Folks at all ages and stages benefit from building that essential base to operate the job hunt from.

Section II The Actions That Work….39

Practicing before you meet the employer will bring back great rewards. By yourself or with a friend these action steps work.

Section III The Person In The Mirror….73

Taking a good look at yourself and what you offer – the good and the wish things were different.

Section IV Winning Steps: Getting the Person in The Mirror Ready…..   103

Have some fun as you put together a full tool kit.

Tips, Techniques and Tools To Master The Hunt

Building on the Basics

Section I   Introduction:

So you are looking for work, eh? You are entering the most frustrating part of the hunt because YOU know that hiring you is a good idea, you just have to find somebody smart enough to agree with you.

And the questions! Your Uncle Fred is asking again "so, haven't got the job yet?" Hang in there because the Job Hunting Tool Kit will give you the means to land that job and to change the way you see the world around you.

Oh, the advice 'do this and don't do that' will not be found here. You need to be yourself and not follow blindly the advice from others who "know the secrets" of what works for you. The whole idea behind the Tool Kit is to use the skills and heart already inside of you.

The first guy I ever job interviewed 29 years ago stood a foot taller than I am. He grabbed my hand tightly and shook it hard three times then mercifully let it go. When I stood there letting the blood return to my hand I asked why he did that. He replied "well, I read this book that taught me how to shake an employer's hand".

Tips, Techniques and Tools To Master The Hunt

Folks, you already know how to shake someone's hand.

The Job Hunting Tool Kit focuses on your brains, heart and courage and gives exercises to practice as you get ready for what the future holds for you.

Section I

Table of Contents

1A. the Most Essential Step:

Where to Put Your But

1B. Comparing Yourself to Buddy

1C. Introducing The Job Hunting Oz factor

1D. Teaching Aliens About Baseball

1E. The Sad, Sweet Truth about George Herman Ruth

1F. Yes, the Libraries are Full of Them

1G. Breaking News: Millions of Worried Bees Falling From the Sky

1H. The Tale of the Chicken hawk

1I. Following Your Passions

1J. Building Your Cheeseburger voice

Tips, Techniques and Tools To Master The Hunt

Section I

Table of Contents

1K. Lessons from the Tennis Court

1L. What Three Bricklayers Can Teach You

1M. The Spirit Side of The Job Hunt

1N. Job Hunting Courage As A Small Voice

1O. Diamonds And Coal

1P. Mary's Wisdom: For Those Who Think They Can

1Q. Beating the Top 40

Tips, Techniques and Tools To Master The Hunt

The Most Essential Step:
Where to Put Your But

One of the greatest first steps in job hunting is learning where you put your but. (That is with one t in but… this is a family oriented book after all.) Stop for a second and listen to that internal conversation every job hunter has – where the real battle for success is won or lost.

> "I really want that job … but… I have this problem."   Or
>
> "I have this problem …but … I really want that job."

The problem is either in the macro or in the micro. By macro I mean **the big picture** of the world around you (high unemployment, changes in the business climate, companies leaving your area). By micro I mean the things that effect you *personally* (I have a disabling condition; I am too old or fat or ugly for the job).

In facing this question, it does not matter if your problem is big and impersonal or small and really personal, placing your but in the way of success

Tips, Techniques and Tools To Master The Hunt

stops you before you even get started.

Think about that for a moment. It is very easy to watch the news and decide that times are too tough and how are you ever going to make it in times like these? THAT emotion will show itself in your walk, in the way you talk and will sap the energy in your smile and your style.

SO WHAT! When you hear 20 jobs were lost across town, SO WHAT! You aren't looking for twenty jobs, you are only looking for one person smart enough to see the energy and spirit inside of YOU and hire YOU. Lose that spirit because of something outside your power to change things and it will show up and have the energy slowly leak out of your energy balloon.

Now the micro side of things where you take a look at yourself in the mirror and do not like what you see. Yes, I would like that job but come on, I am just too darned (fill in the blank) to get hired. Folks, you have just fired yourself before you even had a chance to get hired.

You are much more than your disability or shortcomings – you are a valuable person and could become the employer's valued team member

Tips, Techniques and Tools To Master The Hunt

if they could see past the problem, right? Well, first YOU have to see past the problem to seeing you as part of that team. As the job hunter THAT picture in your mind is the most powerful thing you have going for you. Use it, do not lose it.

How you phrase the 'but' question determines your ultimate success. If your but comes before your 'problem', the last thing you think of is why you will NOT get the job. You have built a mountain to climb even before you get to the employer, whew! Isn't it harder to go into the interview that way?

Putting the 'but' after the problem puts your desire and drive first.

Hey, think of these things from the employer's point of view, **who would you hire**?

Remember that the person with the self-*confidence to land the job despite barriers* is the employee who will solve problems at work with ease and confidence as well.

FREE HELP:

Every county in the United States has what is known as a "One Stop" where you can learn of the

Tips, Techniques and Tools To Master The Hunt

full range of governmental help (resume writing, practice interviews, etc.) you have available to you. Learn more about this by going to www.servicelocator.org and find the range of services available to you right now.

Making It Work:

Write down all of the things that are in your way in your job hunt, listing them as macro and especially the micro things affecting your hopes for your future work. Make it a long list **(25 or more)** and include some silly things like how it is bound to rain on workdays and you may get Darth Vader for a boss as well as personal things like I am pretty old or I have this prison record.

Be honest and true to yourself.

Which ones of these are on the right hand of the 'but' sentence and which ones are on the left side? Be painfully honest with yourself because this IS all about you after all and if you are not honest you are only cheating yourself.

Sit back for a moment and take a look at the sentences where the problem stifles your chance

Tips, Techniques and Tools To Master The Hunt

for getting the job. Your tough chore here is to change your perspective on these issues to saying Yes, I have that problem, but I still want the job more.

Tips, Techniques and Tools To Master The Hunt

Comparing Yourself to *Buddy*

You have great gifts and talents inside of you. For those of you thinking hey, George, you don't KNOW me, how can you be so sure? I know because I know "Buddy".

Compare yourself to a 'blank slate', my favorite fictional person, Buddy - - a person without ANY real skills or motivation (OK, he knows how to breathe in and out, but that is about it.)

From the days I taught preschool kids, I have loved the lazy bones who *is* "Buddy". Take a moment and picture him, folks. He quit school the minute he could and has since only hung around watching television, not developing any work skills, responsibilities, social skills or hobbies. Now down to business...

Tips, Techniques and Tools To Master The Hunt

FREE HELP:

If you have a disabling condition for which you get Supplemental Security Income (SSI or Social Security Disability (SSD) and you want to work but are afraid of how income can hurt you… don't worry! Contact www.social security.gov and ask them for "The Red Book". In the pages of this essential resource, you will learn of the work incentive on everything from extended periods of eligibility to the PASS Program to something called IRWE's.

Making It Work:

Below write down 25 ways you are different from Buddy. For the more advanced version, compare yourself to a 'Buddy' at your job, school or neighborhood (Hint: you can spot him pretty easily at work, he acts so much like the potted plants in the lobby). *Need help?*

Tips, Techniques and Tools To Master The Hunt

** Write about **ways others have given you responsibility** & you have performed well.

** List skills you have gained, from playing guitar to cooking to not mixing darks & lights in the laundry.

** Abilities for **dealing with people**, from selling cookies at fundraisers to giving compassion to others in their time of need.

** Ways you have *proven* being trustworthy (honest), loyal & brave (such as how you meet and beat the challenges you face each day).

** List how you have worked independently meeting goals/responsibilities.

** How do you respond to the needs of others?

** How do you turn pressures into opportunities for yourself and others?

Remember when you babysat the terrible Tanner triplets and you all survived the night? Or when you had to learn about new medications your

Tips, Techniques and Tools To Master The Hunt

grandmother was on so you could better care for her? Or that school project you completed with others as a team?

Have fun letting your mind wander when building your list. Compare yourself to that co-worker who **never** helps train other employees, **never** works overtime on short notice or working with difficult clients. Keep in mind, how are *you* different from **"Buddy"** and do not worry about being too full of yourself because you are comparing yourself to a blank slate after all.

Let your imagination roam to areas that may not seem job related, but that show your character and skills.

Once you have listed the first 25 examples add 20 more.

Tips, Techniques and Tools To Master The Hunt

See? You already have capabilities making you valuable and different from others. These **unusual** characteristics set you apart from your job hunting competition, especially the aspects which raise your Oz-nicity (see Oz-nicity in later chapters.)

Keep this list handy, it will come up again in the Tool Kit and in preparing for your future. Onward!

My 'Buddy' List

_____

_____

_____

_____

Tips, Techniques and Tools To Master The Hunt

Tips, Techniques and Tools To Master The Hunt

Tips, Techniques and Tools To Master The Hunt

Introducing
The Job Hunting Oz factor

Each job requires a combination of brains, heart & courage (hey, folks who have seen the **Wizard of Oz, do you** see where I am going with this?) Though they may not call it Oz-nicity, employers want to know the right candidate has:

BRAINS -- *The ability to learn complexities of the job so they can perform them at the speed and effectiveness they need the employee to know it.*

Most applicants do not know what is needed to be known for the job (example: how to make a **Chicken Supremo Sandwich** at Burger World). They DO need to demonstrate that they have the capacity and interest to learn what is needed to be known.

HEART - - *New workers will interact with the job's stakeholders and clients...do they have the heart to deal with them (from the quiet of a library night security guard to the crazy life of a political campaign manager)? Do you have work/life experience to show you have that?*

Tips, Techniques and Tools To Master The Hunt

By stakeholders I mean the people who are an important part of the job like the people you will interact with directly (customers, co-workers, the boss, the public.)

COURAGE - - The toughest for an employer to tell about is the candidate's **courage** because nearly every candidate is practiced in s*ocially appropriate ways* of answering the questions. *Here an employer wants to know that when the going gets tough the new employee will not run away yelling "let me out!" and that he takes responsibility for his mistakes and learns from them.*

Also the boss knows that the employee will work just as hard and effectively at the start of the shift as at the end of the shift and just as well on days she is feeling well (the sun is shining, no aches or pains) as when she is not (trouble at home, a sore knee and it is raining outside).

Making It Work:

Get the list you made when you compared yourself with Buddy.

Put each answer into the category of an example of *head, heart or courage.*

Tips, Techniques and Tools To Master The Hunt

Now that you are connecting the lists together, try to add more examples of how you have brains to learn things, the heart to get along with others & the courage to work while fighting the dragons you face every day.

Tips, Techniques and Tools To Master The Hunt

Tips, Techniques and Tools To Master The Hunt

Teaching Aliens About (Baseball)

When I explain about finding your Oz factor, many people get all worried and humble. **"Golly, George"** they say, "I'm not smart at all, **how can I tell the employer I have the brains for that job**… I will never get hired; I should just go home and eat worms". I normally say "Stop! Really? Worms?" followed by "if you do not know that you have the brains for the job, you are already as good as fired for a job you have never even applied for."

Here is a quick way to have the confidence that you have the brains in something you enjoyed learning or had to learn in order to survive.

FREE HELP:

The internet offers you great ways to show you have brains. For instance MOOC's or Massive Open enrollment online courses give you the chance to study any of the dozens of courses available from colleges and universities from around the world – FREE! Complete a course of two in a field of interest and you can gain knowledge, confidence and a piece of paper saying you have some smarts … just like the Scarecrow in the Wizard of Oz. Just do a search on a list of MOOC.

Tips, Techniques and Tools To Master The Hunt

Making It Work:

Pretend that a Martian has come to earth and says to you in whatever accent Martians have "hey, tell me about this ***baseball*** you earthlings have." Or maybe it says "tell me about this thing called makeup" or "tell me some things about music, eh?"

Quickly write 12 things you know about baseball (famous players, some of the rules, etc.), makeup (brand names, where/how applied, etc.) or music (styles, singers, instruments, etc.).

OK? Now write down twelve more (the survival of our planet depends on it, folks.) Now finally add five more.

Now you have one impressed Martian in front of you saying

"WOW! You know a lot about baseball/ makeup/ music... *you must do that for a living.*"

The morals of this story are that

- if you can learn that much about something **that does NOT pay the rent**... think of how you will make yourself learn about things (like operating a cash register, learning a computer program, caring for elderly patients) **when it IS for money to pay the rent**.

- It is already inside you, folks. The other moral is that if you can talk baseball with an alien you can

Tips, Techniques and Tools To Master The Hunt

talk about yourself with anyone who today is a stranger and tomorrow may become your employer.

Tips, Techniques and Tools To Master The Hunt

The Sad, Sweet Truth About George Herman Ruth

In his time, George "Babe" Ruth was one of the greatest and one of the worst ballplayers in the USA. Sure, he held the record for most home runs -- many people remember pictures of him standing alongside home plate *watching yet another shot fly over the outfield wall.*

There are also pictures of Babe walking back to the dugout after just striking out... again. You see the "**Sultan of Swat**" was the *greatest striker-outer* of his era, too.

Think about that for a moment. The Babe *could have* walked around with a mental picture of himself booming homers and had great confidence every time he played. He could also have pictured himself and the hundreds of times he would walk sadly, slinking back to the dugout after 'striking out, again. *It is all just a matter of perspective.*

In job hunting you are facing some of the things the Babe felt. Throughout the hunt you have faced **disappointment** and you have enjoyed some levels of *success* (hey, you knew enough to get this book, right?)

Tips, Techniques and Tools To Master The Hunt

It is all up to you and how you look at yourself in the mirror. Remembering your homeruns is a *whole lot more fun,* more satisfying and gives you more energy than dragging your feet and keeping the picture in your mind of striking out again. When meeting an employer, picture yourself cracking a home run. It'll show in your stride.

Tom Edison, inventor of the incandescent light bulb, tried & failed ***over 2000 times*** to put together what later was one of history's greatest inventions. Asked what he learned from months and months lost time and failures, he said "I learned 2000 ways not to make a light bulb." *It's all about perspective.*

Making It Work:

Take a moment and draw *two pictures of yourself.* In the first draw a picture showing you *doing something you have accomplished* (*learned, did, and met an important responsibility*). Now write a caption describing the picture and what you are thinking at the time.

Under the other draw a picture of you accomplishing something **you want to be doing someday**. Now write a

Tips, Techniques and Tools To Master The Hunt

caption about how you are feeling about doing that someday soon.

Hey, **HAVE SOME FUN** & draw the pictures. It's OK to erase and rewrite, ***but please have some fun***. Make them things you will enjoy remembering in the days ahead when you hit home runs and make the occasional strike out. Remember that **your life is** an unfinished 'picture' with many miles to go and lessons to learn.

Picture #1

Picture #2

Tips, Techniques and Tools To Master The Hunt

Libraries are full of them

Did you know that **Babe Ruth** grew up in the Pigtown section of Baltimore and that all but one of his siblings died before they reached their teens? In the orphanage where he grew up, the brothers taught him first the trade of becoming a shirt-maker and only later taught him to play this new game of baseball.

Or **Mary Kay Ash**, who as a single parent raising her kids in the Great Depression mixed soaps in her bathtub to make ends meet? She later became the leader of one of the world's largest beauty services companies making Mary Kay cosmetics.

That **Michael Jordan** was cut from his freshman high school basketball team before deciding he would try again instead of thinking that basketball was a dumb game. That **Walt Disney** was fired from his first job at a newspaper for not having enough imagination? Yes, **that** Walt Disney.

There are thousands of stories about people who had every reason to crawl into a ball and never become a success. But they became successful anyway.

Most of the important work in the world is done by people who are too tired, too disabled or too something else to do it… but they did it anyway.

Whenever you feel that you are just grunting through

Tips, Techniques and Tools To Master The Hunt

another useless day and that success must be meant for someone else, just remember that **the libraries are full of stories** of those who faced harder problems than you have now and they made it to a brighter future anyway

FREE HELP:

Libraries have great resources in learning of biographies which will motivate and inspire you. Most libraries have agreements with other municipal libraries where you can borrow books for far away just like it was being borrowed from your hometown. Look up online the biographies on Wikipedia.org Give it a try!

Making It Work:

In your spare time, take a moment and write down the names of 10 famous people you respect. Maybe they lived centuries ago or are living right now; just make sure that it is a list **personally** important to you.

Now go to your library or do an internet search find a biography of a few of the people on your list. List below a copy of what their resume would have looked like before they "made it".

Like Al: at age 13 his family moved Italy after his father's company failed due to new technologies, Al stayed back in Germany. He moved to Italy by quitting school with a medical excuse. He renounced his German citizenship to avoid military service, earned a degree in teaching but was unable to find a job in the field for years (by now he had a

Tips, Techniques and Tools To Master The Hunt

wife and two children.) In his early twenties he landed a frustrating job as an assistant examiner in the Swiss Patent Office, all of this preparation for becoming the Albert Einstein he was meant to be. As Albert put it himself

"Life is like riding a bicycle. To keep your balance you must keep moving."

Take the time to read about them and the challenges that they faced. Jot down some notes that will help you in your search, ideas that will help you weather the darker, cloudier days in your job hunt.

Tips, Techniques and Tools To Master The Hunt

Bees Can't Fly:
The real birds & bees story.

Yup, there was a theory for years that **bees could not possibly fly**. Scientists and other really-smart-people considered that such round, tubby creatures with those itty-bitty wings can't physically or aerodynamically fly. But they do, because nobody told them they can't. If somehow we would get word to the bees that they cannot possibly fly and that they should just stop trying, then millions of bees would suddenly fall out of the sky never to fly again.

It was discovered in the 1990's that bees actually had adapted a way of beating their wings that was unique – not up and down but in a circular motion that made what had been thought impossible to be possible.

Do you ever hear that there are things you can't do because you are too short, fat, old, dumb, poor or just too (fill-in-the-blank)?? Others say the same sad things over & over to you or worse yet, maybe you are saying them to yourself. Repeating these lies about who you are

Tips, Techniques and Tools To Master The Hunt

and what you are capable of can limit you so that you may never "fly" to where you are capable of.

Back to my original point – if bees didn't fly, think of the flowers that would never get pollinated, the honey that would never be made – **we are all better off because bees do not worry about what they "cannot" do and adapted a new way because they thought they CAN.**

How about you? The world would be a sadder place if you do not take the steps to be more than 'they' (or you) may think you can become.

Speaking Frankly:

My high school friend Frank had a problem. He wanted a sail off into a career, but his guidance counselor kept saying no. Frank just had to aim lower. He wanted to apply to Marquette University but the counselor said it would only frustrate him to get rejected. Avoid the frustration he was told and just aim lower.

Frank told me about the conflict he faced - that he had one thing in his heart, but the counselor must know something he didn't know, *he was the expert for crying out loud*. But Frank followed his dream.

Tips, Techniques and Tools To Master The Hunt

It had been years since I had seen Frank when we met last year. He was the same affable guy I knew growing up and he never did go to Marquette he joked. Maybe he would go visit the campus when he retired from the Navy.

Ooops, forgot to call him by his title, Admiral Sciortino. He got there by listening to the one expert about Frank who would always be with him, **Frank himself.**

Making it Work:

What are 3 stories you know of where "everyone" thought something would happen and it did not? It does not matter where the story comes from – politics, sports, weather.

Now write them down. What are three stories you have heard affecting other people where there were supposed limits people broke through?

What are three things you have heard about your limits? Write down these 3 supposed limits – through the Tool Kit Series you will have fun proving them wrong. Before we move to the actual work, please remember something I tell others at the groups I run: **"Every great idea that ever**

Tips, Techniques and Tools To Master The Hunt

was started with someone dreaming it and a thousand other people saying 'Are you crazy?'" Keep dreaming.

Tips, Techniques and Tools To Master The Hunt

<u>The Tale of the Chicken hawk</u>

There was a woman walking through a forest when she found a baby eagle on the ground lost from its nest. This woman lived near a family of chicken hawks so she brought the eagle to live with them and to be raised by the chicken hawks.

For months, the little eagle learned the ways of the chicken hawk, a bird that knows well how to peck at the ground and *<u>to just survive</u>*. One day the baby eagle saw an adult eagle flying gracefully overhead. He said to his brother chicken hawks, "wow, what is that?" The reply was "Oh that is an eagle, the most beautiful bird around here, flying when and where it wants to." But don't waste time thinking of that because you are just a chicken hawk."

The baby eagle kept thinking about that bird he saw and began working to be more like him. As he started running and falling down then flapping his wings and falling down again, the other chicken hawks mocked him. As he tried to stretch out his cramped wings, they said he was doomed to fail, asked why he was shaming himself and his family, making a fool of himself and wasting his own time over and over again.

But with each attempt he became stronger and more assured that he was doing the right thing. With time he

Tips, Techniques and Tools To Master The Hunt

began to fly – a little at first then more the next day and he became the eagle he always was deep inside.

He never forgot where it was he came from as he would bring back to his family gifts and stories of his adventures – and he would fly like an eagle again.

So now is your turn. Maybe you are like the baby eagle facing people around you who mock your attempts at a better life. Just remember that every great idea (democracy, the pretzel, your goal to land that special job) begins with one person believing it and a thousand other people saying "what? You must be crazy!"

Making It Work:

So what makes you so special, brother or sister chicken hawk? Why are you not satisfied with just pecking at the ground and just surviving? What is the image that you carry for the day when you are flying away?

Draw the outline of a house you want to live in someday in the future and fill in a picture of what you want that house to look like - - including pets, a car or piano or river in the background. Whatever you hope for in that dream even if others think it is crazy, it is your dream.

Write down five things that today are in your way from this dream – like the mocking others may throw at you. Make certain that you do not join in the mocking, but as you

Tips, Techniques and Tools To Master The Hunt

knock off each thing that separates you from the dream, cross out the thing you have listed.

_____
_____
_____
_____
_____
_____
_____
_____
_____
_____
_____
_____
_____
_____
_____
_____
_____
_____
_____
_____
_____
_____
_____
_____

Tips, Techniques and Tools To Master The Hunt

_____
_____
_____
_____

Passions

One often overlooked aspect of job hunting is that you should have something in your life that provides you with ***passion***. Even if it is only part of the job, that source of passion makes the day and the daily grind go easier. It also makes the job interview more fun. (**Yes, I said job interview and fun in the same sentence**.)

For a moment, sit back and dream of what stirs you inside to action or take your attention and time. Take a moment and write down your answers to the following questions:

- Name two things that while you are doing them you lose all track of time.

- When a topic comes up on the radio, TV or computer what makes you stop and listen or read?

- When you were a child, what did you want to become as an adult? Why?

- Many people want to have an 'end product' to their work while others like working with others – which one are you and why?

- Tomorrow you will wake up right when and where

Tips, Techniques and Tools To Master The Hunt

you want to live – describe the scene. Who are you with, where are you and what are you doing for a living?

Now that you have these answers, compare them with the jobs you are going after today. I appreciate that many jobs are there for you to make ends meet, but what is it about the jobs you are seeking that matches, even a little, the things you listed above?

Take your time with this one because when you find the connections, it will allow you to have more of a spring in your step going to the employer – more of a reason to tell the hiring manager that picking you is a good idea because you have a special connection to the job. And that special ingredient is passion.

Tips, Techniques and Tools To Master The Hunt

Using Your Cheeseburger Voice:

One of the great questions you need to answer before hunting is **how to talk with a prospective employer** while making a first impression.

Your tone of voice needs to portray **assertiveness** and self-assurance. Your voice should not sound **pushy** or boastful; be polite and respectful, but not too soft-spoken. In short, be blended like a fine wine (not a whine)**.**

HOW ARE YOU SUPPOSED TO GET IT RIGHT?

First of all, do not buy expensive job hunting books or hire speech coaches hoping that you hit **just the right sound** when talking to the employer. It's already inside of you.

Folks, *you have that voice inside of you* and **here's how to use it**: *Quick!* Raise your hand if you have ever ordered a cheeseburger (or soy burger for our vegetarian friends). **THERE!** THAT is the tone of voice you need!! That

Tips, Techniques and Tools To Master The Hunt

commanding yet friendly tone is what you are hungering for. *Relax* and picture yourself ready to order and **say out loud** *"I want a cheeseburger."* WOW! Say it again, slowly: *"I want a cheeeeseburrrger."*
Hey, you really **mean it**! You said it straight up, plain and seriously. Sounds like you aren't leaving this place without that *cheeseburger*. Hey, *you are not making excuses or apologies for what it is you want* to say. You are not bragging or angry, just direct.

You want to get the right tone in talking with the employer? Use your *cheeseburger* voice from saying hello to getting through the interview:

- it's sensitive without being *whiney*
- it gets your **point across** easily
- it doesn't *frighten* or put-off employers
- it's a well-known and accepted tone and it gets the *burger* every time.

*The **cheeseburger** voice helps you in other areas (like "getting past the bull dog", "ending with a period" and "don't think like a job hunter"). For now, practice it & enjoy it.* **With relish.**

Tips, Techniques and Tools To Master The Hunt

Making It Work:

Practice this tone of voice. Try saying other things you will be saying with that tone, like "I want to see the employer" or "I have the experience you are looking for." Make a list of 15 statements you will want to say to the employer and other statements you want to make to friends/teachers/coaches then practice them with that **cheeseburger** *voice of yours.*

1.)--
2.)--
3.)--
4.)--
5.)--
6.)--
7.)--
8.)--
9.)--
10.)---
11.)---
12.)---
13.)---
14.)---

Tips, Techniques and Tools To Master The Hunt

15.)--

Practice your cheeseburger voice with friends, a stuffed animal, anywhere you can hear the sound of your own voice. More on this later.

Tennis Lesson

This is one of the most frustrating lessons for me to remark about because many feel that they have to become someone they are not when in the interview. The best way I know to express this is to mention how I learned of its power.

Years ago I was playing tennis against an old friend and his serve would fly past me every time. I took him aside and asked *what his secret was* - - did he inhale or exhale just before hitting the ball? He thought it through and each time in the next game he served the ball he was concentrating so much on whether or not he was inhaling, his serves slowed enough that I was able to hit them back.

Once he noticed how concentrating on something that really did not matter was affecting his game, he laughed out loud and shouted "it just doesn't matter". He then went back to being himself and firing those laser serves that I just watched as they flew by.

Remember that man a foot taller (and a foot wider) than I am grabbed my hand held it in a vice grip shook it hard three times then let it go. When he noted "well, this book I read said grab the employer's hands…" I told him next

Tips, Techniques and Tools To Master The Hunt

time, "just be yourself".

Making It Work:

Think through the physical part of the interview. What advice have you been given or what parts of it have you become worried about?

Certain parts are essential – making sure that you are looking good, smelling good with an authentic smile for the person who is taking time out of their day to meet with you.

Most employers are anticipating that people have some things that make this meeting less than the real person – hey, you are giving your best first impression. The key to this is to make certain that you are being yourself and not constrained in ways to act that are not you.

Make a list of the different parts of the physical aspects of the interview (eye contact, shaking hands, posture, etc.) and circle the ones that you are concerned with. Now think through what it is that you want to do about them and consider if that is something you will be comfortable doing.

_____
_____
_____
_____
_____
_____

Tips, Techniques and Tools To Master The Hunt

_____
_____
_____
_____
_____
_____
_____

Tale of the Three Bricklayers

Employers usually believe they are better than average *judges of character*. Part of their assessment of YOU is if you consider their agency's work

1.) important to you and

2.) theirs is a place you will stay for a while.

Knowing how they may 'size you up' helps you prepare for meeting with decision makers. A good way to understand this is the **Tale of the Three Bricklayers.**

An opinion surveyor walked up to three people 'laying bricks' on a work site and asked each of them "what are you doing?"

The first one growls "I'm slapping two bricks together, then another and then another ...what a stupid question!"

The next one states "well, we're a team. I build a wall, she builds one and he builds one".

Tips, Techniques and Tools To Master The Hunt

The third smiles and said "Thanks, I am helping build a cathedral people will enjoy for generations to come."

The moral is that they are doing **the same job** only looking at it differently and it shows in their attitudes. Take a moment and reflect on the *attitude* an employer looks for in longevity, solid customer service & other intangibles for the job he is filling. **Will he find it in you?**

FREE HELP:

The internet has many programs which operate as "interest inventories". They ask a range of questions about the things you enjoy doing asking you to rank how you feel about different things to do. Complete one and see if you learn anything you may not have known about yourself.

Making It Work:

Now reflect on how you are feeling about each job you are considering. Would you see the work as "slapping two bricks together" or as something more?

Nearly every job offers the chance to see the work as larger than 'just bricks" but it's up to you how you will see it. Make a chart with 3 columns: "just bricks", "team work"

Tips, Techniques and Tools To Master The Hunt

and "cathedrals" adding your thoughts on each job you are considering and which column they belong in today.

On another day, without looking at today's list, write down your thoughts a second time. This helps focus your mind more fully. The employer will see your true attitude pretty quickly in how you present yourself your answers and that look in your eye.

Tips, Techniques and Tools To Master The Hunt

Spirit

In all of the books I have read on job hunting few discuss the spiritual side of the search. I do not mean a religious matter – just keeping your spirit and motivation 'up' while you are doing the soul sapping struggles you face. Remember in the job hunt that you take time for yourself to appreciate the beauty around you. For example that you

- See the beauty in things not necessarily man-made, but things like sunsets or the beauty in the night sky.

- Find yourself a safe place where you can focus on the things important to you.

- **Put together a box that is all yours with things that give you a sense of peace – from photos, to things you enjoy doing to scents that you like.**

- List traditions that bring you peace of mind (such as saying thanks daily or playing favorite music)

Tips, Techniques and Tools To Master The Hunt

Getting used to feeling centered is like learning to get your balance or riding a bike. Before you can move forward with confidence, you need to feel sure of your balance. Also, balance requires moving forward with confidence.

Making It Work:

Here is something that can help you through the hunt – and often it is free. *Build a centering box* – put in a box or in the bottom of your sock drawer where you can.

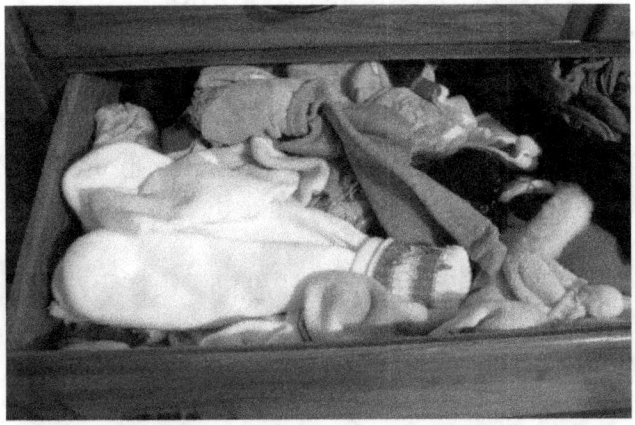

Keep things in a private and safe place the items and images (sensory things) that help you feel more centered and at peace. Write down a list of what goes into that box.

Appreciate nature every day. Find something in the world around you that has its own rhythm (from the last song of the birds before sunset to the rattle of a passing subway car). Write a list of these things and add to the list you find as days go by. Write a list of traditions you have enjoyed that give you a sense of warming your spirit.

Tips, Techniques and Tools To Master The Hunt

Courage – a small voice

Sometimes you feel so small as you look for someone smart enough to hire you. More and more you face the idea that the future will never look anything different from the present, slogging through more days like the day before.

The tough part here is that the winner in the job search is often the person who projects a positive image – how to do that when the days are all so gray? This is when you appreciate that sometimes courage is not about bravado, but is a small voice that says "well, I will try again tomorrow".

Margie's Courage

Years ago I counseled a young single mother of several children. She cried in talking over the lack of job skills she had because she *was just a mother*. **She had heard of the lines of mothers being coaches and nurses and she was not buying those as job readiness skills. She needed to understand something more specific to HER life.**

Tips, Techniques and Tools To Master The Hunt

We spent hours talking about the Headstart program her children were in. This preschool program required that parents get involved and she elected to join committees like the ones that put together the holiday parties for the kids.

Mary joined this committee and quickly noticed that when she spoke, *other people listened* and they appreciated her insights. She showed them the energy and positive spirit that made her a successful single mom as she headed up several projects. Even though teachers or administrators had sometimes in the past made her feel small and relatives had questioned her parenting skills sometimes, here she learned to have courage of her convictions and to be heard.

Soon afterward she became a supervisor in a local hospital dietetics service. Her kids are doing fine having a great role model for learning their own courageous side.

Making It Work:

Think of a saying you have heard in the past for motivation. Ask around to friends or look into it yourself – but make certain that these nuggets have meaning to you.

Return to the lesson "Libraries are Full of Them" and make a list of people you know – family, friends, teachers. What makes them unique and special in your estimation?

Now take these things that are special to you and write

Tips, Techniques and Tools To Master The Hunt

them down – say them loudly when you feel your spirits waning. Otherwise, you can find three quotes from your research on motivating for a brighter future and read them aloud at the start and end of each day you are job hunting.

A Diamond is just a piece of coal that did well under pressure

You never really know about a person – especially their courage and character – until you have seen them handle pressure. It is only then that you see if the person remains a lowly piece of coal or becomes the diamond that lies beneath. Remember that a diamond is just a piece of coal that did well under pressure.

In the Job Hunting Oz factor we focus on the quality of courage. Note that the more you are able to present courage – ability to work well under pressure just as well on good days as bad – the more you are able to show your diamond-like qualities. But first YOU have to see it.

Making It Work:

List the challenges you have faced in the following four sections.

Tips, Techniques and Tools To Master The Hunt

A – **In your studies**. Academic counselors say it is not the super high school student who does well in college, but one who knows how to handle it when she cannot understand something easily and works hard to get it all learned.

B – **In dealing with or helping others.** How do you handle clients/customers who are difficult to deal with?

C – **In the decisions to do the right thing,** especially when what is right is not easy.

D – **In dealing with your own personal challenges**.

Let your mind drift through some divergent thinking searching the ways you have become the person you are. And remember that courage and conscientiousness is not all about brave actions… it is often just a small voice inside.

- Is there anything facing you now that challenges you to move from a piece of coal to a diamond?
- Facing challenges in the four sections noted above – how are you planning to address them now?
- What are your plans for what is next in your personal challenges?

Now use some convergent thinking and find the top answers to the above questions to show not just yourself but the stranger who will one day become your next employer. Hey - and enjoy yourself.

Tips, Techniques and Tools To Master The Hunt

Those who think they can

She was a single mom back in the Great Depression, a time when there were not many supports for families in her situation. She began making then selling soap she would make in her bathtub with the little money she could put together.

Well, she got pretty good at selling and **with hope, hard work** and the help of others she created one of the largest cosmetics companies in the world and named it after herself, **Mary Kay** Ashe. She regularly stated that one of the keys to her success is a phrase she never forgot:

"Those who think they can, can.

Those who think they cannot are right."

The point here is that it is essential you think you can accomplish something in order to finally do it.

Tips, Techniques and Tools To Master The Hunt

People who question if they can are no less competent, smart or capable of meeting the goal. What holds them back is that they deep down do not think that they can make it. Think of the successful people you have heard of, met or read about. They all shared Mary Kay's secret.

Making It Work:

Review the Oz factor and review what you have in the way of brains to learn things; heart to get along with others and courage to be conscientious and honest in growing with time.

You are still in the process of growing your Oz factor, growing your smarts, your heart and your lion-ness. Review your answers to the first lessons, circle the ones that give you confidence that you are going to make it.

These are the sides of **who you are**… not someone else, not some model from another job hunting book but YOU.

Write these answers in the space below and once a day before you start the day's job hunt say out loud **"those who think they can, can, those who think they cannot are right. I think I can."**

Tips, Techniques and Tools To Master The Hunt

Beating the Top 40.

Somewhere near you is a radio station where you can still hear the top forty songs either of this week or a week years ago. The reason I focus on 40 here is that it is an easy number to remember and use and because I miss the show "American Top 40".

Take a moment because you are up against a lot of competition for jobs. OK, have already figured that one out, but know also that many people who do not prepare well for the hunt will soon fall of and no longer be your real competition.

Making It Work:

Tips, Techniques and Tools To Master The Hunt

Below are forty X's (competitors for a job) and one O (that's you). Now cross out a few X's the competition who have not examined their skills, a few more who have not considered the employer's point of view, a few more who became discouraged while you kept on moving forward.

Keep this chart as you complete the JHTK crossing out more X's as you learn more about language, other job search fine points and so on. Once you are done, you will see that your real competition is not as big and bad as you first thought.

X X X X X X

X X X X X X

X X X X X X

X X X X X X

Tips, Techniques and Tools To Master The Hunt

X X X X X X

X X X X X

X X X X X

O

Tips, Techniques and Tools To Master The Hunt

Section II
The Job Hunting
Tool Kit

Strengths From Within - Your Actions In the Job Search:

The Actions That Work

Section II: *Introduction*

Now that you have the basics of the Job Hunting Tool Kit (JHTK) down, it is time to practice the essential actions you take in moving toward your dreams. This book is action oriented reviewing how to address the situations you will face but this time you face them in the straightforward JHTK way that emphasizes your personal strengths.

Know that the smartest thing that you meet today can do is hire you before someone else **does**. THAT stride, THAT look (and the dozen lessons from this book) will get you the job.

Tips, Techniques and Tools To Master The Hunt

Table of Contents

2A. The Oz Factor – The Employer's Point of View

2B. A first Step – How to Define "Janitor"

2C. Nobody Buys the Nova

2D. The Difference Between Sizzle and Steak

2E. Impressing at the Teddy Bear Interview

2F. Getting Past the Bulldog

2G. Building Your Own Bull's-eye

2H. Learning From A Lumberjack

2I. Fighting Groundhog Day

2J. Boats facing the waves

2K. Moving Your Locus

2L. Spirituality

2M. Sharing Through Volunteering

2N. The Importance of an Interest inventory

2O. Walk with a purpose

2P. Nobody Can Make You

Tips, Techniques and Tools To Master The Hunt

Employer's Oz

Now that you have learned of the OZ factor, we need to see it from the employer's point of view.

As you know from the first section of the Tool Kit series, the Oz factor is based on the idea that employers are looking for people with

- The brains to learn how to do what the job requires with the efficiency and speed that the job requires.

- The heart to get along with the people you will interact with either directly (customers/clients/co-workers) or indirectly (stockholders, neighbors).

- The courage to do the job without people questioning your honesty or your commitment to doing the job right.

Most employers do not assume that you will arrive on the first day knowing all you need to know to do the job well… **training and practice are important** parts about learning the job. The question is do you have the experience to learn it relatively quickly or the ability (the brains) to learn it without bankrupting the company to teach you.

When it comes to heart, employers like to know that you have the ability to get along well with the people they HAVE to get along with – maybe you have similar experience or can relate to the social demands you will face on the job.

Tips, Techniques and Tools To Master The Hunt

Courage and your conscientiousness is the hardest for the employer to gauge but ultimately one of the most important qualities and one that most folks either have or they do not.

The lesson is to understand the Oz factor that employer will base her decision on when considering your application.

Making It Work:

Write down your top four prospective employers, listing underneath each one the words the employer's Oz factor. Beside each of them, write the essential parts of

Brains (what is to be learned, taught, done on the job);

Heart (what kind of people will be served on your job, how you will interact with co-workers or customers)

Courage (what are examples taking responsibility for your mistakes and learning from them that the employer would find interesting?)

You may not be able to make a full list the first time out on this exercise, so feel free to return to this one as you get used to it and learn more about the employer.

Tips, Techniques and Tools To Master The Hunt

Tips, Techniques and Tools To Master The Hunt

The "Janitor" Game

When I started in the placement field I was asked to get a janitor for a specific employer. I had just the right person for the job, I thought. He had talked of years he has spent cleaning in places just like this employer wanted. I placed this perfect person knowing I had done the greatest of all placements in the history of placements. Ooooops.

The employer called me and through his laughing he insisted that I send him a **real janitor**. When he caught his breath, he noted HIS definition of janitor included someone who knew how to run a buffing machine. Apparently, the first time people use a buffing machine it tosses them around the room – which is what was happening to the poor person I sent in to that job.

I found through that unforgettable time that it is the definition of the job from the employer's point of view (POV) - that is the only one that really matters. You may have some great skills but unless you are speaking the employers language it is all for naught.

FREE HELP:

On-The Job Training Program and/or Wage Subsidy incentives for employers give hiring managers powerful tools in hiring someone and getting help paying their wages while you are in training. Since you are most expensive to an employer while you are learning the job, these incentives give you the chance to get hired while you learn.

Tips, Techniques and Tools To Master The Hunt

Ask your "One Stop" center for more information on this one.

Making It Work:

Use divergent thinking and write a list of the jobs you have done like how your experience is different from 'Buddy' (see JHTK Book I) a person who has never done anything since leaving school. For example, if you have worked extra hours when asked, completed training or helped others with training them, ass that to your list.

Review the type of work you have done as if the person you are describing it to has **never** done that work before.

If you cared for elderly patients, did you take vital signs? What do you mean by helping with hygiene? Did you ever work with groups of people? Make this part of the list as extensive as you can.

Once that list is completed, review it for each employer you are hoping to work for. Different employers will look at your experience differently, so mark up the different aspects of your experiences keeping in mind their POV.

In the end it is THAT POV that lands you the job.

Tips, Techniques and Tools To Master The Hunt

Tips, Techniques and Tools To Master The Hunt

Nobody buys the Nova

Years ago, the **Chevy Nova** was selling fast in the United States, but unable to sell well in Mexico.

Hey, this is the NOVA! It's a great family car, looks good, runs well ... *even looks good standing still!* But Novas were not selling in Mexico. The 'really-smart-people' who are paid lots of money to solve problems like this tried all the usual methods of raising sales but *nothing worked*.

Finally, Mexican consumers were asked 'why not buy the Nova? *Just look at it standing there in the showroom*!"

Local folks explained that "va" means **go** in Spanish and "no" means **no** or won't. *Nobody wanted to buy the car that* (in their language) *was the* **'Won't Go'**. The 'really-smart-people' then gave the same car a new name and *blamo*, sales soared.

In a similar way, remember to *speak the employer's language*. Words that may be simple and easy for you to comprehend may be considered differently by the employer.

Tips, Techniques and Tools To Master The Hunt

Remember how once I placed a person in a job as a **janitor** because he said he had some related experience. (Hey, 'janitor' seemed like an easy job title to fill). The employer's definition (the one that **really** matters after all) "janitor" meant someone with experience with buffing machines and the person I sent to him did not.

Learning their different language has more benefits. Your experience that may at first seem unrelated can be matched to their language: Experience as a waiter may indicate skills such as training others; working extra hours on short notice; working as a team member; providing customized customer service or responsibility for handling money.

Expand the range of what you say you have done because a little title can mean big responsibilities in their language, but you may need to practice describing it.

Making It Work:

Review your resumes for words you use to describe work you have done. Just as "janitor" has different meanings to different people, other job titles/responsibilities you have had may not reflect the range of work you have done.

Tips, Techniques and Tools To Master The Hunt

Make a list and *circle* words you are currently using in your resumes/applications/verbal descriptions about your skills and responsibilities. Now on a separate page write about your work in *action verbs* (training, writing, selling, and supervising) and look for how you can add the action verbs to your resume/application/descriptions with words particularly of interest to the prospective employer. In her language, eh?

Informational interviews with an employer, just for asking what kind of characteristics she looks for in an employee, help you appreciate her 'language'.

Tips, Techniques and Tools To Master The Hunt

The Difference Between Sizzle and Steak

Version One:
"Mirage" Hickey sits impatiently while people hover around her, smearing acrylates copolymers, salicylic acid, octyl propenamide copolymers and alpha hydoxyl acids on her face while others aim a machine that blows *scalding* hot air at her head. She then walks to her job where strangers shout and grab at her legs and hands.

Version Two:
Beautiful Mariah Carey gets the royal treatment of top makeup artists and their *colorful* wares, while stylists prepare her *soft* hair for the *roaring* crowds at her latest sell-out concert.

I am describing the same reality, Mariah getting prepared for a concert, but one is the nitty gritty (the steak) and the other is the **excitement** you can related to (the sizzle).

In describing **your** experience and skills, make certain to talk of the *sizzle* using words they can relate to and paint a word picture of how their life will be easier with you as an employee:
** the customers will be happier
** work will get done without worry
** you will be reliable and fun to work alongside
** the employer's boss will be glad he hired such a gem.

You can see how this goes- - **you** are sold on the future all the time. Burgerworld does not focus on telling you how cows are raised for their burgers, instead telling you how great they taste and how you will love them once you give them a try. Even eating more fiber (that tastes like

Tips, Techniques and Tools To Master The Hunt

cardboard) is good because it will make your body trimmer and sexier. How do you sell *your* sizzle?

Making It Work:
Return to your **commercial** and description of skills. Do you emphasize how you will do a great job and make your employer's life better?

Think of examples how your brains, heart and courage will help you do your job to make the *customers better*; the company *reach its objectives* and *employer's life easier*. **You** have to see this future before you can describe it and have the employer see it.

Use as many sensory images and as many examples as you can. Write the points you want to express below.

Tips, Techniques and Tools To Master The Hunt

Teddy Bear Interview.

In preparing for meeting an employer, we are working toward knowing what to say and finding the right way to say it. Now practice hearing the words which come out of your own mouth. Just you, and your teddy bear.

Yes, it *is* best to practice in front of a mirror or with friends who will tell you the truth (like 'sit up straighter' or 'you really sounded like a dweeb then') . But it is often best to find someone first who will not criticize you too harshly (hey, he's made of fluffy stuffing after all).

Here is an old friend who patiently listens without correcting you so you can hear your inflections and uneasy silences as you prepare for the interview. He will sit there looking at you with soft eyes, soft ears... just soft all over.

I recommend the teddy bear method early on as it *allows you to try & fail* without criticism. And after you gain confidence, it dawns on you that you are, well, talking with a stuffed animal. If you can do that well, you are ready for practicing with live people and for the other tools in the kit.

Tips, Techniques and Tools To Master The Hunt

FREE HELP:

Talking to your teddy bear or the air gives you the valuable experience of hearing your own answers to the questions of the practice interview. Be assured that when you are talking aloud that you are not just "talking to the air", but are connecting to a side of yourself you may not have appreciated thus far.

Making It Work:

Practice your commercial and the 3 main questions (Why should I hire you? Why would you work for me? And tell me why you are the best candidate?) with a stuffed animal.

Tips, Techniques and Tools To Master The Hunt

Tips, Techniques and Tools To Master The Hunt

Beat The Bulldog

She stands there, guarding her turf. And you are going to get past HER? HAH! Many have tried & failed, *slinking back home*, unable to get past her and to that goal of so many others before... to meet the employer.

Ahhh, she is very good at being a bulldog guarding the employers time and to beat her (or him) you have to learn to think like a bulldog. **This dog knows two rules**:

- The boss doesn't want to be disturbed, so don't waste his time with bad applicants.
- **Never forget rule number one.**

A bulldog needs to know whoever gets past her must be worthy of the employers time and attention and that FEW people meet those qualifications. If she lets the wrong person by, the boss will remember her mistake long after the boss has forgotten the name of the bad applicant.

Every error she has made is like a scar embedded into the bulldog's tough skin. The dog now squints into horde of job hunters and vows "I won't get fooled again."

Tips, Techniques and Tools To Master The Hunt

How will YOU get by? By out-thinking the code of bulldog-nicity.

1. **Be politely insistent**: Practice your cheeseburger voice & be genuinely polite, respecting the valuable time of both bulldog and employer. This can be a refreshing change from the others busy trying to see the boss.
2. Practice saying "that's OK, I'll wait" to bulldog-isms like: "She's in a meeting, a looong meeting" or "we are not hiring at the moment" or "we close for business in half an hour". The dog may not know if there *is actually* an opening at the present time, but just using the line 'we're not hiring' to get you to leave. That's when your 'that's OK, I just want to shake her hand' works well.

   1. Get an informational interview. Here you do not apply for a specific job, you only want to hear the employer's opinion on what kind of person he/she is looking for or info about the employer you can't get in the traditional ways. Hey, it works because as the saying goes, for many

Tips, Techniques and Tools To Master The Hunt

people there is no sound quite as sweet as the sound of their own opinion!

Get creative: One candidate sent a shoe shaped candy dish to the employer saying "now that I have my foot in the door, let's talk..." One ...ted in a letter that if I have not heard from you by Tuesday at 9 AM I ...ll call then, and then called saying the employer is expecting my call.

Make sure you show respect for their precious time, for their position and that this agency is special to you.

Making It Work:

THIS is a skill you can best develop through practice. Take the list you have of the employers you hope to work for and note next to them the name of that company's bulldog.

With time, make some notes about how you were able to get past the bulldog to finally meet the employer. Practice (and success) will help build your skills.

Tips, Techniques and Tools To Master The Hunt

Tips, Techniques and Tools To Master The Hunt

Building Your Own Bull's-eye

Wow! Days can be *long* out there job hunting. Much of the discouraging part is that things can seem *All-or-nothing.*

Friends and relatives say "did you get the job yet?" (Sounds like finger nails on a chalkboard sometimes, doesn't it?) Or "did you get the interview...yet?" or that sarcastic neighbor Jack who twists his lip saying "so you still aren't working yet, ehhh?"

You're putting in the hard work and hours of making contacts, but still you have to face

Jack –

Here is a way to know you are moving forward even on days you don't land the job.

Right now you have a tiny target that has only this itty-bitty bull's-eye labeled "got the job". Miss that target and you feel like a failure. Folks, let's just make bigger bulls eyes!

Tips, Techniques and Tools To Master The Hunt

Landing a job is really a **series of steps** *where you progressively* ***move toward*** *that goal of the job.*
On to the exercise...

Making It Work:

Make a big bull's-eye covering 1 piece of paper with the center ring saying: "Got the job". ***Now*** *make several concentric rings around it, labeling each a step closer to the* "Got the Job' goal.

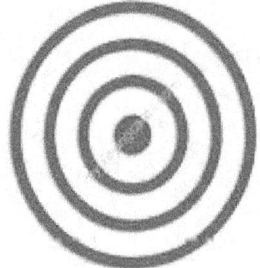

Examples include
** Listing potential employers
** finding name(s) of **person(s)** at the company who can offer job
** getting past the company 'bulldog'
** meeting or writing to the **person(s)**
** building a resume tailored to that job
** other steps, fill your ideas here
Now make a list of **your** ***top employers,*** *giving each its*

Tips, Techniques and Tools To Master The Hunt

own one page bull's-eye with concentric circles and succeeding chores. Put an "x" (and date it) *where you currently stand with each employer* and write below it what your next step will be to move closer to that bull's-eye.

Make plans *each day* (written plans are best) on moving toward the target center with your employers, noting your *progress* with new x's (with dates) put on the targets as you move closer to the bull's-eye.

And smile when you see **Jack**, knowing even if you didn't hit the bull's-eye, you hit the target and are *moving closer day by day*.

My Bulls-eye

Tips, Techniques and Tools To Master The Hunt

Learning From A Lumberjack

One of the most frustrating chores that I have done is chopping firewood. Hey, it is exciting to swing an axe and to eventually turn logs into something more useful in a fireplace.

While you are chopping, you know that with all of the energy used most of the swings do not appear to do anything.

You swing the axe and maybe only chip off a little wood or sometimes nothing at all. It is frustrating, timing and aggravating because on the outside all of that effort is going nowhere. And how about friends who stop by and ask *"how is it going now, eh?"* or watching the time tick by and nothing is happening.

Sound familiar? Job hunting is a lot like that – lots of effort, different swings and still not much happens. And the frustration you feel by the comments of others and the feeling that time is just ticking away.

The good news for you now –

there IS something happening with each swing.

Inside that slab of wood, **things ARE happening**- bonds are breaking and what looks like something you will never crack is gradually breaking free. On the outside, the wood cutter is getting stronger, more determined and one swing closer to your goal.

Tips, Techniques and Tools To Master The Hunt

Again, it's that way in the job hunt. Each swing you make (interview, handshake, phone call) may not yield the visible results you want but each loosens what you may not be able to see:

- Another employer has heard about you.

- You have had other experiences connecting your skills to another job

- **Another person knows that you are out there and ready to work.**

And things are also moving on the outside:

- You have practiced your stride, your "commercial" again

- *You are picturing yourself working*, making the image stronger with practice

- You are one swing closer to your goal.

This all leads me to the description **of the law of big numbers**. Almost any goal attempted often enough comes closer to coming true. Remember the story of the football coach who told his underdog team that yes, they may lose to that other team nine out of ten times… *but who is to say that today isn't that one in ten times that they would win?*

Sales representatives who are told that one in ten phone calls leads to a meeting and one in five meetings ends in a sale are reminded that they get one sale for 50 calls – if

Tips, Techniques and Tools To Master The Hunt

they only call 49 they may miss that sale.

Making It Work:

Make a list of the different chores in the job hunt... making a list of prospective employers, finding the name of the hiring manager at each employer, using ways to contact that person. Now make daily and weekly goals and know that you are going to make them and move forward toward your dreams even when you cannot directly see it.

Tips, Techniques and Tools To Master The Hunt

Groundhog Day

In the great movie with Bill Murray and Andie McDowell, the star has to relive February 2nd over and over until he learns the right life lessons before he can move on. Imagine it, folks - one day just like all the days before. Hey, if you have b0een unemployed for any length of time, you **really** know what that is like.

Bill Murray learns that by being a more spontaneous and giving person he can finally start each day as fresh and different. And there is the lesson for you.

Later the Job Hunting Tool Kit Series, we will discuss the importance of keeping up your spirit and how helping others will make you a more attractive candidate. For this lesson, take a good look at yourself and consider if your life is like just an endless stream of similar days.

Making a change would make you a more interesting person, add to your resume/application and would give you references who appreciate you are more than just a resume.

FREE HELP:

If you earn income and can qualify for the earned income tax credit, you also qualify for the Advanced Earned Income Tax Credit.

What's that? You can receive half of the anticipated tax credit for next year through your current paycheck. This benefit may help make today and tomorrow easier and

Tips, Techniques and Tools To Master The Hunt

different from the grind you face today. Your credit next year would be reduced, but your paycheck today and tomorrow will be fatter.

Making It Work:

Write down five things you have wanted to do for yourself or others but you have not had sufficient time. Maybe it is a skill you have wanted to move on but life got in the way. What is an age group or activity you want to share with other but so far have not done anything about?

Make sure that your list meets three requirements:

- YOU can do this given your time and financial limits.

- It is something that you could interrupt if a job came available next week.

- It adds to your Oz factor brains, heart or courage.

Personally, I would lean toward doing something for others because along with getting good references, adding to all aspects of your Oz factor, it also gives you a good feeling at the end of the day that someone else's day is better off because of you. This can turn any day from the routine… just ask Bill Murray.

Tips, Techniques and Tools To Master The Hunt

Tips, Techniques and Tools To Master The Hunt

Boats facing the waves

In order to survive in choppy water, a boat that steers into the waves stays afloat better than one with its sides to the waves.

Take a moment and think through the challenges that you are facing in the hunt. **When the unexpected happens are you ready or will you be ready?** Are you more apt to React in response to events or will you be ready to act from a plan?

Making It Work:

List the stresses and demands you may face in your job hunt such as the responses you may face in trying to meet with the hiring manager; the questions you may face in job interviewing and related tests (see 'eye rolling' lesson).

Are you prepared for how these may affect you and how prepared are you to move forward in this matter.

Tips, Techniques and Tools To Master The Hunt

Internal/external

A great differences between job hunters is between those who think that life happens to them and others who thing that more often than not, they affect their world even more.

By that I mean there are people with *an internal locus of control* (that the changes in your life start with you and your decisions) and others who have an external locus of control (where the decisions affecting their lives come from outside forces.)

In these days with so many things outside of your personal strengths, it is easy to be an external thinker. As jobs are moved out of your area by people who sit in corporate offices in another state or time zone, it is easy to think that the decisions that affect your life are from the outside.

This lesson is for you to find the parts of your life where your determination calls the shots.

Making It Work:

Write a list of your activities this week, especially as it effects your job searching. **Make it a long list.** Now make a mark beside the things that were your decision to do them, where you had a say in what you did and how you did it. Go ahead and complete this for the whole week, I'll wait.

OK, now review it and see all the times you did things outside of your control did they have a higher purpose like

Tips, Techniques and Tools To Master The Hunt

caring for a child or moving toward a personal dream? Put a notch beside those.

Was it part of a routine that other living and breathing people have to do (laundry, sleeping)? Now make a mark beside them.

Now take a long look at what remains. Is there any way that you can changes what is there to make it more your style? Like working on the resume, waiting to see an employer or filling out an application… think of trying something different next time.

Do something nice for the office manager while you wait in the lobby or put yourself more in the employer's point of view when writing that next resume or application.

NOW you are just a little more in control.

Tips, Techniques and Tools To Master The Hunt

Tips, Techniques and Tools To Master The Hunt

Appreciating Your Spirit

Job hunters often see work as an issue of self-worth and as a deeply personal matter.

Through the ups and downs of job hunting, remember to appreciate *your spiritual side*. It helps to know that you are supported when earlier you were *on the mountaintop* as well as in this valley. You have not been abandoned.

Some people believe in a higher power as that support, others look within themselves.

Either way works if it gives you a sense that you can make it through the tough times.

Anyone can make it through when times are going well; it is only when someone faces up to tough times that you can find a person's true character. Hiring managers appreciate that and they often are looking for the spirit you have in these times.

- Do you blame outside circumstances for your situation, or do you take some personal stake in what you are facing?
- Are you focused on what is in your past or what can be in your future?
- Do you look forward to that future with the sense that you will be alright?

Your response to these questions will show on your face and in your stride as you meet the next employer so make certain to address them *before* the next interview.

Keep a thankful heart and confidence **that each day begins a new morning with its own possibilities**. No thing or event can take hope and thankfulness away from you.

Tips, Techniques and Tools To Master The Hunt

One great way to see the world as full of possibilities is to volunteer. I understand that your financial position may make volunteering seem out of place, but for your spirit and your resume it may be just what you need.

Volunteering provides help in the following ways:
- Spirit: You get a sense that you are needed, valued and productive. Often you can get a sense from watching the reaction and development of others that they see the future as different from the present thanks to your work.
- References: Volunteering gives you the opportunity to get current references from someone who appreciates your work and service and they can give examples that are from right now, not before.
- Resume: Someone is giving you responsibilities you are meeting (courage); you are learning new things and putting them into action (brains) and getting along with people well (heart).

"Making it work" focuses on 'the joy of service' how that will work for you and reminding you of the Russian sailors saying *"Pray, but keep rowing to the shore."*

Making It Work:

This is three parts –
- Be honest with yourself, how can you improve your faith and hope for your personal future? What are ways you can move forward positively?

Tips, Techniques and Tools To Master The Hunt

- Make a list of volunteering opportunities you may have in your community with agencies that would not have political reputations that may affect your employability with some hiring managers.

- What do you see as the benefits to you personally in volunteering in your community?

Tips, Techniques and Tools To Master The Hunt

Volunteering

You can't get the job without experience and you can't get experience without the job, eh? You want a current reference, who will praise your brains, heart and courage, but you can't land that first job? Each day ends as frustratingly as the last one ended as you keep looking for that job?

Yes, I talked of it in the last lesson, but it can also help you out here. It can be the solution to each of the questions in this lesson – *volunteer!* Here you have the opportunity to find **something fulfilling to do** which will indicate to prospective employers that you have a heart for caring for others and the best part is you can often call the shots as to your availability.

People having trouble making ends meet may feel that volunteering is a waste of time. *Please look past this* to see that the benefits are much larger than you may first consider. If you move on this matter, make sure that it will be something you will proudly describe to another person.

FREE HELP:

Your local United Way or related agency keeps a thorough account of the community needs and may have a roster of places in your hometown who could use a volunteer like you. Contact them and learn things about your community that you may not know and also learn how you can be part of the solution to a problem in your own neighborhood.

Tips, Techniques and Tools To Master The Hunt

Making It Work:

Once you have figured that you want to volunteer as a way to enhance your skills application and resume, ask yourself three questions:

- Do I prefer having a completed 'object' at the end of the day, or is working with others satisfaction enough?

- Is there an age group or type of individual that I get along with best?

- Is it an organization that will not mark me as a certain sort of person (strong political leaning, negative local image) to someone who does not know me well?

From these three questions, get in touch with your local volunteer center or United Way to find someone who needs your skills and interest. Yes, you will go through an "interview" before being placed for the position, but here is an organization that values you for who you are and what you can offer, not seeing if you meet certain qualifications for a specific duty.

THAT can warm the heart of any job hunter.

Tips, Techniques and Tools To Master The Hunt

Interest Inventories

An effective, fun way to focus on what you would like to do either in paid work, hobbies or volunteering is taking an interest inventory. It can be helpful and easy but can also be manipulative and sometimes dangerous. More on that **'dark side'** later.

An inventory helps you move from the thousands of choices you have of possible for work & play to narrow down and spotlight those you have a *particular interest* for. It narrows by giving you a selected list of dozens of different jobs and activities then asks you to rank each on a scale of Really Love to Really Hate to do it.

Inventory results can especially help those at a *'crossroads'* (students, seniors, and people ready to change careers). The inventory clarifies jobs or hobbies most in-line with your stated interests.

Now the bad news:
Inventories are subjective and boy can they be manipulated! If you start with an idea of what you want the inventory to say about you, *voila!* THAT is what it will say.

Tips, Techniques and Tools To Master The Hunt

For example, if I was 'cooking challenged' (word is that I am) but want others to think I should become a chef, from my 'votes' an overall picture of interests is developed and gosh darn it, says I should be a chef!
Big bold letters and everything... just couldn't prove it to others -- like the guy at the pizza shop who says 'Pepperoni, extra cheese again, George? Your night to cook, eh?"

The inventory measures interests, not skills. You can fool the inventory; *just don't wind up fooling yourself.* A danger can arise if you live your life according to test results. Hey, if you want to be an artist, but the inventory, your wallet or job prospects say something else, enjoy artwork as a hobby because "interests" need not mean a career.

Go after your desires and avoid the regrets of a dream never chased. As the great hockey star Wayne Gretzky said, "you miss 100% of the shots you never take."

Making It Work:

Visit your local 1-stop employment office or go online and take an interest inventory; answer questions from your gut, quickly. **And have fun.**

Tips, Techniques and Tools To Master The Hunt

From the results, make a list of work, hobbies or volunteering related to your listed interests. Follow up on these prospects with a list of places to pursue your interests and enjoy finding your true interests.

Tips, Techniques and Tools To Master The Hunt

Walking With a Purpose

In working at placing people through an employment service (or as a job hunter yourself) it is REALLY important that you **understand the kind of person** that the employer wants. Although there are many insights found in the JHTK series, this one is special.

Let us go back in time to one particular employer I went to meet and learn of the kind of person she wanted as an employee. I had been warned that this one hiring manager was nicknamed "**the female Darth Vader**" the ruler of her own empire, **the Personnel Department**.

Through our meeting, she talked on about the people "who just did not work out". When I asked her to describe the kind of person who DOES work out, she abruptly stood up and said "follow me".

She quickly walked ahead of me, pointing out this machine and that warehouse dock, not introducing me to anyone. As we sat back in her office I repeated my request, "describe the kind of person you want." She looked at me with the withering stare Darth would have she said,

"I am looking for someone who walks with a purpose, someone who when they tour the plant *walks with that purpose.*"

THERE was the lesson – and I have seen it in every employer hire ever since. From the employer's Point Of View (POV), you want someone with conviction in their

Tips, Techniques and Tools To Master The Hunt

demeanor and their stride. People can hide part of the personality with practiced phrases, but put them in a position where they have to show real confidence and that is where you find the people who stride.

As I have heard many times before – "you can't teach drive." You either have it or you do not.

Making It Work:

Take a walk. Do not be self-conscious about it, but try to walk with a purpose. Similar to the Cheeseburger voice where you talk with purpose, put that into your stride.

What is your purpose in that walk? What is your purpose in getting the job? To make new friends – provide for yourself and family – build something special?

Take a few moments and just people watch for a moment in your hometown. Now pick out the people who walk with a purpose and those who do not – it is not hard to tell the difference.

Write down the purpose of your walk and remember it so it will show in the way you walk. Tap into your inner Luke Skywalker or Princess Leia and walk.

Tips, Techniques and Tools To Master The Hunt

Nobody can make you feel inferior

Eleanor Roosevelt spent most of her public life talking about empowering the people who did not feel they had power or respect. Like her or not, the wife of Franklin Delano Roosevelt was certain of what she was saying. One of her most famous quotes goes like this…

"Nobody can make you feel inferior without your consent."

Think about that for a moment.

Other people and their biases, difficult circumstances, challenges that you face – especially self-inflicted problems such as substance abuse – each of them can conspire to make you feel "less than" other people.

"How can I measure up to other's expectations?" "What would they think if they knew 'the real me'?" "How can I compete with people who are younger/faster/stronger/skinnier/etc. than me?"

You **KNOW** you can because you are the most important person and have the opinion most important to your success.

Tips, Techniques and Tools To Master The Hunt

FREE HELP:

If you are the victim of harassment or abuse, there is an agency or maybe more with staff who are there to help you. You do not deserve to be intimidated into silence or the feeling that you are 'less than'.

Do not wait, folks. A brighter future begins with a call to your Social Services office or house of worship. Ask about your nearest 'sanctuary'.

Making It Work:

In what areas do you feel 'less than' your competition in the job hunt? List them and be brutally **honest** with yourself.

Now review the list and consider if each one (one at a time, folks) is a realistic reason for being considered 'less than'- or not? Is there some where you are allowing yourself to feel inferior when in fact you are not?

Is the reason someone else's (a friend, a parent, society) bias? If it is realistic what can and will you do about it? Share your answers with someone you respect and every so often, ***especially at the end of a long day***, repeat Eleanor's quote. Out loud.

Tips, Techniques and Tools To Master The Hunt

The Job Hunting Tool Kit

Section III: Strengths From Within – The Person In the Mirror

Introduction

When building something special you have the rough work of creating the foundation the rest of your actions will rest on – but you live best when the fine work is prepared. Through the Job Hunting Tool Kit series, we have focused on how to tap what is inside of you and move forward toward building your dreams. The basic skills and actions are in place and you can stand proudly in what you have built so far.

- **Your cheeseburger voice factor**
- Finding Your Sizzle stuffed animal

* Growing your Oz

* Interviewing with a

Now is the time for learning the tools that provide you with ways to deal with the predictable and the unpredictable. You gain confidence that whatever you face; you have the abilities and the tested tools to meet the challenge. This is the difference between wanting and getting that job.

Tips, Techniques and Tools To Master The Hunt

Table of Contents

3A. Oz-nicity: Intermediate Lesson: The Oz Factor
3B. What I bring to the Employer
3C. You are Who You Are/ Ain't Who You Ain't
3D. Before You Leave Your House - Adjust your words
3E. Questions You Need To Prepared For (and more)
3F. Dealing With Stress Interviews
3G. Be Careful To End With a Period
3H. When Their Mind Wanders
3I. The Unasked Test - Eye rolling
3J. Dealing With Your Ugly fish
3K. Lord Churchill - - *You Are Drunk!*
3L. Never teach a pig to sing
3M. IPS – How to Eat A Cow
3N. Informational interviews
3O. Failure is not a person/ I never lost, only behind
3P. Building Your Spirit/ Making Yourself More Interesting
3Q. The Big Battle lines: Frosting versus Cake

Tips, Techniques and Tools To Master The Hunt

Oznicity

Employers are looking for essentially the same thing, no matter their area of work...

** Do you have the **brains** for the job?

** Do you have the **heart** to deal well with the customers and "stakeholders" of our place of work?

** Do you have the **courage,** honesty and conscientiousness to handle each day well, accepting blame when it is rightfully yours to take?

Well, fans of the Scarecrow, the Tin Man and the Cowardly Lion, we are looking for the brains, heart and courage found in Oz... **and in you as well**. Everyone has brains, heart and courage already and with help can show them to others. (Sounding like a wizard a bit there, eh?)

Show you have brains! An employer's unasked questions here are:

Have you ever had to learn something quickly and/or thoroughly? In your work here, you have to learn how we do business; *do you have what it takes?*

Tips, Techniques and Tools To Master The Hunt

Have examples ready even if they at first seem distant from what the employer does, it will prove to him or her you have the smarts.

For instance-- maybe you have never used a cash register, but you are comfortable with computers and can show what you know.

By heart: The unasked questions include: Can you get along with the customers we serve on good and bad days; can you mix in well with the different kind of people already working here? Can you have the right mix of compassion and toughness needed to care for our customers/clients here? What are some experiences you have had that show you have the heart?

For example – you may never have worked with the elderly, but you have cared for your disabled relatives and can give compassion to those different from yourself.

And courage... Like telling the truth when a lie would be easier or being reliable when you could find an excuse for being 'off that day'. Employers wonder will you be just as reliable on a good day as on the days you do not feel well?

Tips, Techniques and Tools To Master The Hunt

Do you have honesty where I can trust you to do the right thing when no one is around to watch? Will you accept blame, correction or criticism when you are in the wrong? Can you give examples/references on this because just words are cheap?

> For example—name the greatest stress/failure you have faced? How did you deal with it and learn from it?
> How did you work it as a food service clerk when other staff left with the flu in your busy season?
> Did you work the late hours to finish that report with the impossible deadline?

Every job from grave digger to CEO requires certain Oz Factors. As you learn what the employer wants and what you have to offer, use the Oz factors as your guide. Know how your brains, heart and courage match their needs and be ready to show your factors, proudly.

Making It Work:

Pick your top four employer prospects and write down, from their perspective, what are the essential Oz factors they want: what abilities to learn (biology, selling tactics, how to build a sandwich?), 'heart skills' (getting along,

Tips, Techniques and Tools To Master The Hunt

challenges on a bad day) and courage (what if you make a mistake, can you take it?).

After that is completed, compare your factors with their needs. Amend your factors as needed; looking for gifts/talents you had overlooked to match what they are looking for.

Tips, Techniques and Tools To Master The Hunt

Oz factor: what I bring

This is where you can connect your Oz factor with the concerns of the employer's Oz factor needs.

You have already considered all of the things that show you have the **brains** (things you have already learned, examples of how quickly and thoroughly you can learn things and can put things into action) **heart** (how effectively you deal with helping clients and customers as well as co-workers and supervisors) and **courage** (how well you learn from your mistakes, giving "an honest day's work" every day).

You have also considered the concerns perspective employers have in finding their next employee.

- **Brains** to learn the job (has the applicant learned similar things in the past? How well?)
- **Heart** to do the job (can they handle the social stresses of the job well?)
- **Courage** (can I walk away for a while and know the job is getting done as I need it to get done every day?)

Now combine the two lists because this is where the employer figures if hiring **_YOU_** is a good idea.

Tips, Techniques and Tools To Master The Hunt

Making It Work:

- Set up the two lists side by side.
- Circle places where your factors and skills match the employer needs, even if they are not exact.
- Look at the materials you are currently using in your job hunt (resume, interview preparation, applications, JIST cards) and see if you are emphasizing the areas you have just circled.
- Write out ways you can emphasize these points of your OZ factor and their Oz needs and integrate them in the new, improved materials.

Tips, Techniques and Tools To Master The Hunt

Adjusting Your Words

All of the pieces are there now to rewrite your resume, applications and JIST cards to best present yourself to any employer.

The employer has a special way of looking at the job (the Employer Oz factor), you have a set of brains, heart and courage that you can continue to develop (your own Oz factor) and you appreciate the importance of finding the right language to meet the employer's perspective (Nova, Janitor and other chapters). Now we bring these all together.

Just a reminder on what is a **JIST** card. People you are competing against have experience and training appropriate to the job but that gets lost in all of the reading the hiring manager has to do.

In order to stand out while showing appreciation for their time pressures, give the employers a snapshot of your best qualifications related to the job and their specific perspectives on a 3 by 5 card.

CHEAP HELP:

JIST Cards give you the opportunity to keep your name in front of the employer and to spotlight the points you want to make. They also give you the opportunity to show the employer that you value their time by putting what you want to say in bite-sized morsels.

Tips, Techniques and Tools To Master The Hunt

Get yourself some index cards and work with your friends on what to say knowing that you are the expert on YOU.

Making It Work:

Get out your resume and applications for your top four employer prospects and circle the verbs in them. Also review the points you are making about your accomplishments.

Get out your answers to earlier "Making It Work" exercises on your Oz factors (your brains, heart and courage) and the employer's Oz factor (the type of brains, heart and courage they are looking for). Being true to yourself, are the specifics in your verbs and statements appropriate to the Oz factors involved?

Change them where they are not. Are the words used what they need to hear and are you clear in how you say it? Are they prioritized with your important points in the first spots and either bold or underlined to emphasize those points?

* note that sometimes, putting strong selling points at the end of a section can draw an employer's attention as well.

-

Tips, Techniques and Tools To Master The Hunt

- _____
_____
_____
_____
_____
_____
_____
_____
_____
_____
_____
_____
_____
_____
_____

Tips, Techniques and Tools To Master The Hunt

you R who you R

Growing up one of my favorite songs was sung by Arlo Guthrie and it was about letters sent to an advice columnist, Dear Abby. Take a moment and catch some of the lyrics:

> Dear Abby, Dear Abby, my feet are too long
> My hair's falling out and my rights are all wrong
> My friends they all tell me, they're no friends at all
> Won't you write me a letter, won't you give me a call
> Signed Bewildered

> Chorus: Bewildered, bewildered you have no complaint,
> You are what you are and you aint what you aint.
> So listen up buster and listen up good,
> Stop wishing for bad luck and knocking on wood.
> Signed, Dear Abby.

> Dear Abby, Dear Abby, you won't believe this,
> But my stomach makes noises whenever I kiss.
> My girlfriend tells me it's all in my head,
> but my stomach tells me to write you instead.
> Signed, Noise-maker.

> Chorus: Noisemaker, noisemaker you have no complaint,
> You are what you are and you aint what you aint.
> So listen up buster and listen up good,
> Stop wishing for bad luck and knocking on wood.
> Signed, Dear Abby.

Tips, Techniques and Tools To Master The Hunt

Folks, it is as simple as that – you are who you are and you ain't who you ain't. Yes, people do change and grown and education can make you more marketable, but the faults and weaknesses you have are part of who you are.

Tell the world that although you are working on your imperfections, you know what they are. The best way an employer can hear of how you face adversity and meet it is in your descriptions of your flaws and how they make you unique and special.

Describing your flaws benefits you from the employer's perspective because; from her point of view your description –
- Gives a fuller picture of who you are (there are so many people well-rehearsed in what to say, it is refreshing to get the real news.
- Let's the hiring manager know that you see yourself with some honesty.
- There are fewer surprises on the job when problems inevitably arise.

Making It Work:
Make a list of the habits you have that make you less than perfect. Now ask two other people whom you trust to make a list from their point of view of your imperfections. Tell them you want them to be brutally honest and you don't mind what they say (and mean it).

Tips, Techniques and Tools To Master The Hunt

Sleep on it one night then take a good look at the lists – these will give you a good amount of information describing that you are who you are and you ain't who you ain't.

Avoid taking this personally or permanent, but know that it is truthful and will give you some honest answers to "tell me about yourself".

See the commercial and the 3 questions in other books in the JHTK series.

Tips, Techniques and Tools To Master The Hunt

3 questions

In all of the interviews you will have through the years, there are three questions that are either asked directly or indirectly and your being ready for them will put you ahead of the people who are not ready.

Tell me about yourself...

The employer is giving you the opportunity to connect what makes you special to the demands of the job open. It is important that you take this opportunity to talk first of all what makes you different and how that difference makes you a good fit for the job.

Make certain that you are brief and focused in this question because rambling on about unrelated things ("I was born in a log cabin on the banks of...") will make the employer's mind wander and when they wander, they normally wander away from you.

Why should I hire you?

This is where you can make an image of your working there and to transfer that image to the employer's mind.

Take all of the reasons you have why hiring you is a good idea and boil them down into four or five central points.

Essentially you are showing how you are a better selection than others who may also be interviewed and that you have the essential ingredients (the Oz factor) for the job at hand.

Tips, Techniques and Tools To Master The Hunt

Why do you want to work for me?
The employer is really asking "hey, we are real strange folks here and we have some tough pressures on us. Do you know what you are getting into and will you have what it takes to stay here?"

The related question is "hey, I am going to invest a lot of time, energy and personal pride (you are the best person for the job in my estimation after all) in you - - are you going to stick around?"

Making It Work:
List the three questions and leave LOTS of room for your answers.

Now list as many ideas as you can to address each of them.

Next step is to consider your top four prospective employers and put a number (1 through 4 for the employers) by each idea which will work from the employer's POV.

You will want to have four to five points to make in answering each question and you will want to also practice saying them aloud so you hear how they sound and if they have the ring of being 'you'.

Tips, Techniques and Tools To Master The Hunt

Tips, Techniques and Tools To Master The Hunt

Stress Interviews

People are *often so rehearsed* in what to say and how to say it in job interviews that they need new ways at getting at what "is underneath".

Admiral Hyman Rickover was in charge of promoting Naval officers during wartime and he faced this problem every day. In order **to get at the real personality underneath** the practiced answers, he perfected what has become known as the stress interview.

For example, Rickover would bolt a chair to the floor and ask applicants to move it over to his desk to start the interview. He had many of these **"props"** (gluing a pen to a desk and ask to have it passed to him, having applicants sink into soft chairs before his desk so he would look downward toward them, etc.) so that the applicant never knew where the challenge would come from.

Rickover would study the applicant's verbal and non-verbal reactions to the unexpected and consider them as a sign of the real person underneath the practiced facade.

There are dozens of ways an employer can throw you a curve during an interview. Be prepared and be confident for getting through the rough spots and to understand that the employer just wants to see the real you.

Making It Work:
Before you do your next practice or mock interview draw

Tips, Techniques and Tools To Master The Hunt

up five questions (or better yet, have friends draw them up) covering the following:

- How would you handle the following problem at work? (Form a question which includes four problems all happening at the same time).
- What is the worst part of the prospective job and how would you handle it?
- What was your greatest failure at work and what did you learn from it?
- Role play with an obnoxious or inattentive client or customer.
- Have your friend invent a few challenges for you in the environment of the interview (noises, interruptions, seating arrangements, and off-beat questions asked). Have fun with this one.

The best part about mock interviews is that you can get all the tension and preparation without the stakes being as high as in an actual interview.

Tips, Techniques and Tools To Master The Hunt

End with a period

Growing up with my big sister, we had that sibling rivalry thing down pretty well. One day we were drying dishes together when she dropped a dish (*kblambo*) and it shattered on the floor. *Sh-sh-sh-shoomph* she flew out of the kitchen like a low-flying jet.

I bent over to pick up the broken dish when my mother walked in, angry about the *kblambo* she heard from the other room. I explained to her **with no real energy or conviction**"well, my sister did it... She dropped it... really...?"

Though I knew the truth (complete with sound effects), when I explained it, it sounded like I wasn't sure...? **Like maybe I was making it up...?**

How does this help you? Before seeing an employer, **review what you plan to say** about your skills/experience that will make you a valuable employee. **Practice it out loud** making certain you end statements with a period. **Like you know what you're talking about** because you know you better than anybody else.

Tips, Techniques and Tools To Master The Hunt

Remember: whenever an employer's mind wanders, it wanders away from you. When something is open to misunderstanding NOT in your favor, that's generally the direction it will go because the employer tries to avoid *guessing* and tries to never guess wrong about hiring. If you leave room for **mind wandering**, they will *wander away* from positive thoughts about you.

How to keep them from *wandering?* **Know your points** and express them with a period. Only way to that is practice out loud.

Making It Work:

Review your Oz-nicity, your answers to the three main questions, your commercial, other aspects of the interview and sound confident, out loud with what you have to say. Practice three times on three different days to get it right.

Tips, Techniques and Tools To Master The Hunt

Tips, Techniques and Tools To Master The Hunt

Love that eye rolling

This is my favorite because the unprepared fall for it *every time*.

You are the employer for a moment... you have a job that requires a *go-getter attitude* and ability to do things and change plans on short notice. You want to avoid anyone who would utter the words "**I'm not going to do THAT**". What to do? **Use an eye roller!** Most of the time the eye-roller is a job related test sprung on the applicant at the right moment.

So you have completed the interview and the applicant has begun to relax. Their guard, up for most of the meeting, is relaxed now and you may see the real person behind the well-rehearsed mask some wear at an interview. NOW!! **HIT THEM WITH THE EYEROLLER**!

Give them a job related test, simple math for cashiers, a written test with vocabulary the right candidate should know. THEN I LOOK AT THEIR EYES AND EXPRESSION!

Tips, Techniques and Tools To Master The Hunt

Did you see them roll their eyes and *sigh a 'oh, not a test!' sigh?* Well, they just told you how they deal with the unexpected. And they just lost a lot of their chance at landing this job today. Why hire the *eye-roller* when another candidate may enthusiastically grab the exam, welcoming the test as a way to show their skills?

Back to you being the job hunter... when an employer springs an eye-roller, like a test or a "come with me on a tour" or "I'll bring in another worker for a moment", welcome it and **avoid** the *eye roller expression* that can ruin a good interview in one second.

Making It Work:

What are some unexpected things that can be thrown at you in an interview? Make a list of some off the wall questions (like 'name six people living or dead you would invite to dinner tonight?' what animal most resembles you?) or job related questions (what would you do in unusual situations at work) tests that can be dropped in front of an applicant. *Ask a friend to give you an interview, have them select a few from your list or come up with their own and remember yourtheir thoughts to your reactions.* Remember, the eyes have it, eh?

Tips, Techniques and Tools To Master The Hunt

Tips, Techniques and Tools To Master The Hunt

Taking a long look at your Smelly Fish

Everybody's got a smelly fish. The better you know it, the better you will be at getting him from ruining your life.

First, a story. A single mother was hoping to one day buy a house, but money was always a problem and her dream seemed far away. One day she went to visit a home for sale and was soon chatting with the owner about the financial troubles that she and her children faced.

The owner, wiping tears away, asked her how much money she had with her today. She shrugged and pulled out the $4.00 she had in her pocket. *"SOLD!"* he said.

The woman found he was not kidding and she accepted the house on the owner's one condition, that he would still own a hook on the kitchen coat rack. He was sentimental about it, and the whole house for $4.00? *What could go wrong?*

She was settling in when the former owner stopped in one evening. "Sorry to interrupt dinner, but I want to take a picture of the hook. Can you take a picture of me and the hook, please?" OK, no harm done - the house was a steal...

Tips, Techniques and Tools To Master The Hunt

Weeks later, she was preparing a small party in her place when the old owner stopped by carrying a 40 pound fish. "Yup, just caught it" he said as the fish dripped on the kitchen floor. "Just going to hang it up here on MY hook."

She allowed it, took a picture of the man and his fish and was surprised when the man left the house leaving behind the fish. The former owner just smiled and said "I'm leaving it on the hook. Don't you touch it now because, hey, a deal is a deal...?"

Days passed - the fish remained there, stinking up the whole house. She was reduced to staring at it and saying "a deal IS a deal."

****

Folks, every deal you make and every compromise made carries the *prospect* that you will be left with a smelly fish. Is it the words you have to say to close a deal on a product you aren't sold on yourself? Is it the late hours or shift work that keeps you away from family?

A different kind of smelly fish pollutes your own self-image. What keeps you from your dreams? Down-cast

Tips, Techniques and Tools To Master The Hunt

friends? Fear of the unknown? A condition (physical or mental) you feel that keeps you from advancing? Best to take a good, long look at the fish you have on your hook in the compromises YOU are setting.

FREE HELP:

Employers can receive a large tax credit for hiring people who are members of certain "target groups", (ex. veterans, disabled, single parents and others. Go to www.irs.gov and see if you are one of the Worker Opportunity Tax Credit (WOTC) targeted groups.

Once you know you qualify, make that solid first impression and when the time is right, tell them that the employer may get a fat tax credit for hiring and keeping you as opposed to other candidates.

Making It Work:

Draw a *picture of the house* you want to live in and in the middle of the picture draw your personal smelly fish...maybe it is a whale, or one with thorns and spikes; maybe it is really a lot of little fishes. Name the fish by the thing(s) that holds you back the most. *Keep this very personal drawing aside* and understand the impact that fish has on your life.

Tips, Techniques and Tools To Master The Hunt

In your own time and your own way, figure how to lose the fish somehow and get it out of YOUR house...

My fish:

Tips, Techniques and Tools To Master The Hunt

Lord Churchill, you are drunk

Lord Winston Churchill had a quick wit that helped him dozens of times. He had one famous encounter that helps with your job hunting.

One night he was at a dinner filled with the richest, snootiest people London had to offer. One woman was shocked (shocked I say) to see Lord Churchill having had too much to drink.

She shouted at him **"Lord Churchill, you sir are drunk!"** Winston turned to her and said softly but directly: "Madame, tonight I am drunk and you are ugly. *Tomorrow, I will be sober but you, sadly, will still be ugly."*

The lesson here is that time and effort, painful as they may be at the time, can cure some temporary problems – but ugly stays. Churchill would become clear and sober again, but her 'problem' would remain. How about you?

Making It Work:

List the aspects of yourself that are 'rust' in that they are part of who you are and cannot be painted over or hidden. Be true to yourself –
- Are you a slob?
- Do you have trouble taking orders or correction?
- Do you get into arguments too quickly?

Make another list this time of the lessons you need in order to address the problems you face. What are the things that time and effort can get it done for you.

Tips, Techniques and Tools To Master The Hunt

Now get to work solving it.

Tips, Techniques and Tools To Master The Hunt

Never teach a pig to sing, it wastes your time and annoys the pig

Somethings in life are just what they are. It will snow in my hometown every winter, dandelions growing in my yard next year and that the sun will come out tomorrow.

The important part of this is the lesson comes from this quote. I have faith and hope that with your tenacity and good sense you will land a job that brings you closer to your dreams. But, folks, there are somethings that you cannot change.

It is to save you time and energy (and sanity) I remind you that pig voice lessons are a lousy investment because outside of Hollywood and Charlotte's Web, pigs have a terrible time carrying a tune.

Making It Work:
Time to bring out that beautiful Serenity Prayer:
"Grant me the courage to change the things I can, Patience to accept the things I cannot and the Wisdom to know the difference."

You already have courage and wisdom (you are reading the JHTK series, right) Make yourself a long list of what frustrates you about job hunt. Please make it a long list.

Now break it down into what you can change and what things you cannot. Now review the list a second time and consider what you can't change list again. With time, help,

Tips, Techniques and Tools To Master The Hunt

education, perseverance are there some things in your cannot list that can be changed. I could buy something to get rid of the dandelions or get in snow shoveling shape to prepare for the snow, making it less a problem. **Like Little Orphan Annie sang "maybe what's good gets a little bit better and maybe what's bad gets gone."**

Now take your list of really can-nots, a pen and a roll of toilet paper. One by one, write down the items on your can't list onto the toilet paper. Once the list is complete, one by one tear them off, sink them into the toilet water and flush them away.

Tips, Techniques and Tools To Master The Hunt

How to Eat A Cow

So many things are happening to you all at the same time that it is easy to lose track and feel overwhelmed by it all. The best way I know how to deal with this problem is to learn from what my late grandfather said –

"The best way to eat a cow is one steak at a time."

Hey, folks, you are facing 'a cow' in being unemployed or underemployed. You will remember years from now how you handled the pressures you are facing right now. Well, with apologies to our vegetarian friends, you have to bring that cow down to size.

One way is to label each of the steps separately, as is done in the Individualized Placement and Support model of job hunting. By *breaking it down into its components*, you may be able to have a greater sense of mastery and a better sense of how you will accomplish something toward your overall goals every day.

Making It Work:

List all of the parts of the job hunting process from your point of view:
- Preparing physically: Appearance, transportation, clothes, etc. so you present yourself as energetic.
- Preparing your message: Resumes, applications, Oz factors of you and the specific employer.
- Preparing your research: What are perspectives of each employer, issues facing the hiring managers for today/future, have you kept up with references?

Tips, Techniques and Tools To Master The Hunt

- Preparing for the fine points: Ready for the unexpected, preparing for questions you may face?
- Add here any other preparations unique to your personal situation.

Tips, Techniques and Tools To Master The Hunt

Tips, Techniques and Tools To Master The Hunt

Informational Interviews

So you have tried your best to get interviewed but *cannot get past the Bulldog.*

Maybe you want to show your capabilities but cannot get through to the employers out there.

Or maybe you are trying to get a better understanding of the interests, points of view and Employer Oz factor, but you cannot find out.

One solution to all 3 of these is **the informational interview**. One of the best ways to find out an employer's needs and point of view is to ask one. A great way to express to an employer your skills is to, well, tell one.

Getting that information and exposure can come through an informational interview. This takes some self-confidence to set one up but as with potato chips, once you have finished one you cannot wait for another.

Making It Work:

Practice setting up an informational interview with three companies in the field you want to go to work in. You may not get all three, but keep at it until you meet at least one.

You will need the following:
- **Who, Where and When** – Find the hiring manager at companies in the field you want to work in.
- **How** – Compose a letter asking to meet briefly with the person you have identified at their convenience

Tips, Techniques and Tools To Master The Hunt

whether or not they are hiring currently.
- **Why** – Well, what is YOUR reason? What is YOUR interest in the field – why THIS company or THIS field?
- **What** – Plan ahead, knowing specific things you want to learn about – especially in the point of view of the hiring manager: how do you select the right person? What directions do you see for the future?

The goal overall is to understand more about the field, understand the Oz factor of the employers you are hunting and when that is accomplished to get the word out about your skills.

Tips, Techniques and Tools To Master The Hunt

Spirit 2

It is important to keep your spirit up as you face the challenges of job hunting. Earlier in the series we reviewed some actions you can take to feel more centered or to make your application more interesting, but in the fine tuning we are more personal.

Remember to feel a sense **of gratitude in the gifts that you have** – the gifts of the world around you and the gifts that you have to share with others. It can make a lasting effect on you to make an inventory of what you need to support your personal spirit.

Helping others toward their goals – whether it is helping someone with homework or joining a job hunting support group – can feed your spirit in a unique way.

Making It Work:

Let us address all three-
- Gaining a feeling of gratitude for the gifts you have requires that you make an inventory of these gifts. Take a moment and list gifts that you share with others - - the sunshine, 24 hours in a day and hope for the future for example.

Include the gifts that you have in the main realms of life – your physical body, your intellect, your heart and ability to deal with others, resources to help yourself financially and your spiritual gifts of faith in yourself, others or tomorrow.

Tips, Techniques and Tools To Master The Hunt

- Make an inventory of what you need for supporting your spirit. This is often difficult at first and requires you to consider what faith means to you and how to foster it for the future. Faith in the future, faith in your being able to meet the challenges ahead.
- Help others toward their goals – give them the benefit of your experience, expertise and caring. This helps open things in your life that only come out in caring for others. At the end of the day you will gain a sense that someone else's life is different because you were in it and know that this day was special to you as well.

Tips, Techniques and Tools To Master The Hunt

Frosting and cake

My late grandfather used to enjoy warning me about seeing past the sweet words of salesmen or others who he called *"all frosting and no cake"*.

In job hunting there is a tendency among some hunters to sell all of the sizzle without having any steak to back it up. Employers are often concerned that they may be fooled by an applicant who is just all sweet words (frosting) without a foundation to back it up (no cake). The trick to it is to make certain that when faced with this the employer knows that she is getting cake after all.

How to do that?

First, make sure that in your resume, application and JIST cards that you are **showing the cake**. Detail specifics of what you can do – have proof with statistics, references who will back up the sweet sounding statements you make.

Second, the cake should be inviting to your audience – review the words about your accomplishments as related to THEIR interests (noted in the job description and all that you have found in research.) If the employers want angel food, avoid giving devil's food.

Third, too much frosting makes the employer wonder how deep the frosting goes compared to where the cake begins. **Avoid too much sweetness** by keeping sentences short, resume easy to read and filled with at least some cake.

Tips, Techniques and Tools To Master The Hunt

Making It Work:

Review your resume, application and JIST card in light of the cautions listed above and make the changes as needed. JIST cards? Bulleted points of your best qualities and qualifications targeting what the employer is looking for.

Tips, Techniques and Tools To Master The Hunt

The Job Hunting Tool Kit

Section IV: Getting The Person In The Mirror Ready

Introduction

Now you have learned to use the main tools in the kit but there are important attitudes and understandings to move to mastering them and building your future.

Here we focus on how you see yourself as part of the world around you (ship in port, fearing not to lose) and how to express it (commercial, sights and sounds). There is so much that can make you a different and better candidate that you can do now. So read on!

4A. Any mule can
4B. Cans and the but placement
4C. Fatigue leads to fear
4D. Fear not to lose
4E. A ship in port
4F. Seed packets/Russian dolls
4G. Commercials
4H. Sizzle and steak

Tips, Techniques and Tools To Master The Hunt

4I. Employer sights and sounds
4J. Failure Is Not A Person
4K. I know There is a Pony In there Somewhere
4L. Sand/glass/sand
4M. Spirit/making yourself interesting
4N. The Care and Feeding of References
4O. Dealing With Those Employment agencies

Any Mule:

A sad truth nearly everyone faces is a play on the quote that every great idea starts with a plurality of one. Yes, every great idea (democracy, baseball, the slicing of bread) started with one person saying "hey...I have this idea."

My version of it is

"every great dream starts with the person saying I have an idea, followed by a thousand people asking sarcastically

"what are YOU THINKing?"

Followed by "Your lame brained idea will never work and here is why..."

It's easy for people to find faults or reasons to put people down instead of moving ahead toward a dream. Like the saying goes,

Tips, Techniques and Tools To Master The Hunt

"any mule can knock down a building;
it takes a good man or a good woman to build one up."

Find someone with a lofty dream and be a good man/good woman for them building them up. Be **that** person for yourself. **Few things match the feeling you will get.**

It's so easy to move in the other seemingly safer direction, but remember libraries are filled with biographies of people who should not have made it, but they did anyway.

Folks, be that good man/woman to yourself. Believe in your dream and maintain it despite those who want you to dream smaller. Look at employers, picturing him/her as a guide toward that dream. Know you will make it but it will only happen if YOU picture it first.

A new CEO of a struggling company gave his executives a series of Russian dolls (the wooden dolls that fit one inside the other) before his first board meeting.

Asked what the dolls were for, he said we have the opportunity to hire people smaller than us, fewer dreams and we will grow smaller, like each smaller doll. Or we can hire people who are bigger, dream bigger and move to heights we cannot imagine today.

Tips, Techniques and Tools To Master The Hunt

THAT shows the importance of unleashing talent... it would be so easy to move in the other seemingly safer direction.

One last point, *find someone else* with a lofty dream and be a good man or good woman for them in building them up. **It makes good practice for yourself** and few things will match the feeling you will get.

This isn't really the exercise. But please think of someone who has an idea or dream that you can be of help with. Sit down with them and discuss how their dream is possible and help them move toward it. Later, talk with them of your dreams and see what happens next.

Making It Work:

Take some quiet time and make a list of negative things others have said toward your dreams. (Or the "***Watch where you put your but***" exercise.) Put it in this formula: *I have this dream* **BUT** (fill in the limitation or excuse here.) Now on another page, write (The same excuses)

Tips, Techniques and Tools To Master The Hunt

Example:

Others say: George wants to play the guitar, but he never has time; has no experience; always put things off. I say: I may 'never have time'; I may 'have no experience' and I may have 'put things off' BUT I want to play guitar anyways. And I will! Have some fun, folks.

Tips, Techniques and Tools To Master The Hunt

Success comes in Cans and not in Can-nots.

Often at the groups I run, I bring a can of spinach. Partly it is in homage to my boyhood idol Popeye the Sailor Man (I will wait a moment while those under 30 years old quickly google "Popeye"). Mostly, I bring it to reinforce the saying that starts this lesson.

Before you can actually move toward a dream, you need to **KNOW** that *you CAN* do it.

Need to KNOW that you CAN do it. You already have some experience with that feeling:
- Getting Up to feed a crying baby late at night when all you want to do is sleep
- Completing a term paper in school though you wondered if you could make it.
- Pushing your body to jog that extra block or lift that friend's couch one more time.

Remember the chapter where we reviewed "where to put your but"? There we reviewed the huge difference in the sentences

Tips, Techniques and Tools To Master The Hunt

"I want that job BUT I have this thing in the way." Versus "I have this thing in the way BUT I want the job".

Return to your answers for that exercise and look at them with a 'can-do' perspective.

Making It Work:
Make a long list of all of the impediments between you and the job you want. Make a map with where you are now marked with an X and where you want to be marked with an *.

In between these markers write down all of the obstacles in your way from achieving your goal (I only have lousy clothes; I have this medical condition; there is no reliable transportation).

Write these obstacles (at least ten) on a LONG list on a separate piece of paper. Now write beside each one of these on your list what you need to do to get past them. Write what you CAN do.

Now when you get to the obstacle you will be ready with how you CAN do.

Tips, Techniques and Tools To Master The Hunt

Tips, Techniques and Tools To Master The Hunt

Fatigue Leading to Fear

The great Green Bay Packers coach Vince Lombardi talked often of how he would prepare his teams for upcoming games noting once that

"Fatigue makes cowards of us all"

When a person becomes tired physically, or emotionally, they tend to not take that extra step, that extra action that they normally would have otherwise.

Think of it in your own life. When you faced fatigue, it is human nature that you did not take chances or shake that extra hand or make that extra phone call. The way Lombardi sees it this is a sign of fear and a loss of opportunity to build a better future.

Making It Work:

Take a look at yourself for a moment and *consider how fatigue has affected you in the past* – the way it makes you less apt to move forward. How can you avoid that?

List ways that you can take care of yourself better physically, given the demands on your time. What are the things you have been meaning to do for your exercise, diet or sleeping that you have not yet put into practice?

Tips, Techniques and Tools To Master The Hunt

By seeing the effect that putting these things off, maybe you can take the time now to make the changes that you have needed to do.

Tips, Techniques and Tools To Master The Hunt

Fear not to lose

The Fulton, NY's G. Ray Bodley High School wrestling team had **won the state title** for three years in a row thanks to the innovative coaching of the high school staff and the building of everything from the mat rats program where elementary school kids learned the basics of the sport to having the best amateur wrestlers of Europe to come to their little burgh to wrestle the high schoolers.

Fulton's matches became 'the place to be' throughout the long winter months – complete with new uniforms that glowed in the theatrical lighting when they were introduced at the start of each match with the strains of Queen's "**We are the Champions**".

Little by little, something arose on the team that led to the loss of their state champ's status. Players started to worry about losing, they became *careful not to make the mistake* that would lead to losing points, losing a match, losing that image of being invincible.

They began fearing **not to lose**. This led to worrying about all of the little things that they did and all of the preparation was lost in anxiousness. Once this snowball began rolling downhill, it gathered momentum and G Ray has not won the title since.

The lesson here is not about reading up too much on what

Tips, Techniques and Tools To Master The Hunt

to do or the tennis court lessons, it is about maintaining a sense of pride and stride and being careful not to lose it.

So We Introduce 'Pigs with Wings'

My co-workers always kid me that I will imagine people landing jobs before they do, joking that a certain person will land that job when pigs fly.

I have found that fearing not to lose stifles some of these dreams before they are allowed to grow. That is why I have begun the Pigs with Wings award. We have a ceramic pig with little cotton wings pasted to its back and people who have the courage to try and who can also avoid the fear to lose and thus remain themselves win the award no matter how long the job lasts.

Here's one to start for your own collection:

Making It Work:

Walk around for a little while with a sense of purpose. Select four jobs that you are being considered for and **make a list of the reasons why YOU are the right person for each job.**

Tips, Techniques and Tools To Master The Hunt

*Read them out loud because the more senses you use, the greater you will be able
to remember each point that you have made (writing for feel, read aloud for hearing and seeing –
I have not figured out yet how to smell or taste the list).*

Now draw a picture of yourself working at these jobs. Have some fun and do not worry about how it looks, this is your drawing after all, as this will help add more of your brain involved in the sense of your being a success.

At the Job:

Tips, Techniques and Tools To Master The Hunt

A Ship in a port...

In the late 1980's a woman who had risen high ranks in the US Navy was about to retire after over 30 years. A reporter interviewing about her work asked 1 question too many...

"Instead of a career, why weren't you home making cookies like other women did then?"

Instead of **bopping him on the nose**, she smiled and replied... *"A ship in port is a beautiful thing, but that is not what ships are made for."*

She then talked of how each individual has special talents & they can keep them in port *with the anchor deep in the water*. They can also choose to do what they are meant for, an adventure of trying out those skills.

You can play it safe and not learn of your talents. Just stay in port where you face rust, cobwebs, boredom and worst of all not reaching for your potential.

Tips, Techniques and Tools To Master The Hunt

Making It Work:

On 3 separate pages write a type of road map for yourself. In the upper right draw a *star* and put by it a description of a dream or goal you have (be as specific as you can be). In the lower left corner write an 'x' and a brief description of your present status toward that goal. Say your goal is to own a car (put that by the star) and all you have saved is $2.25 (that goes by the 'x').

Draw a line connecting the x's and the star and draw dashes along that line. At each dash describe a milestone you will need to reach to finally meet your goal (for example: visit auto dealers; save first $100.)

Now do the same for two more goals and keep updating your road maps as you reach milestone after milestone... and keep your *eyes on the prizes* you have.

My Road Map:

Tips, Techniques and Tools To Master The Hunt

Seed packets/Russian dolls

Did you ever notice how when you go into a grocery store most labels are pictures of what is inside? Before you all give a collective *"well, duh..."* notice one big exception – *seed packets*.

The little envelopes that contain seeds have pictures not of what is inside but *what can become* of the seeds given the right mix of sunshine, moisture and tender loving care.

Seed packets are special that way because the seller and the customer both want the seeds to look like the beautiful, mature grown-ups on the cover.

Hey, **YOU** are that seed! You are always in the process of becoming something more than you are today. Job hunting gives you the opportunity to express to people who are today strangers but may soon become people who pay you for your time and for who you will become.

Making It Work:

Draw three pictures of yourself:
- As a child – including things from that time in your life that were special to you: siblings, games you would play, activities, dreams you had for the future.

Tips, Techniques and Tools To Master The Hunt

- As you are now – including the people, activities and things special to your present day-to-day.
- As you hope to become in a few years.

What have you needed through the years to move toward your present years?

What do you need to nourish the dreams you have for the future? Considering your need for Sunlight (learning, support), Water (resources) and fertilizer (things that hold you over through the tough times)

Ever notice how some gardeners keep the pictures of the mature plants near the plants? Do this for yourself to encourage yourself – like the plants that grow up and be the what was already in their genes.

Tips, Techniques and Tools To Master The Hunt

Building a Commercial

You have just a few seconds to make a first impression and yes, (you know how the saying goes) '**first impressions last**'. People are creatures of habit, often considering your later actions in light of their first thoughts about you.

The more prepared you are for *the first* impression, the better your chance to get the image you want to make.

Plan for how you will address **the 3 top questions** and have them readied in a quick 20 to 30 second commercial. Though you are rehearsing a bit of self-promotion, work at it to come across as non-mechanical, with room to adjust it to your different audiences and situations.

The commercial is about *you* answering '*the mother of all annoying questions*' that goes

> "*so, tell me about yourself...*"

Hey, the employer is not really asking you to tell all about you; only what about you is related to the job. Highlight

Tips, Techniques and Tools To Master The Hunt

for them the *most relevant* info about you first (relevant to your employer's needs – see "don't think like a job hunter") with *supporting information* second.

By being relevant you get their attention, *selling the 'sizzle' then the steak*. Milk advertisers say milk tastes good & by the way, it's good for you. Lead with an example of a skill you have that addresses a central part of the job (you provide an answer to their need).

Next, enhance it with how you have other skills and interests that can help the team as well.
    Like:
I have computer experience and have built spreadsheets for my friends to solve their household problems. I also have experience as a cashier using their computers.

Answer the 2 other main questions the employer has:
** Why do you want to work for me?**
(*Translation: English to Employer-speak*):
I want to know that you consider my place and this kind of work is important to you, **so you will have** dedication to understand the hard-to-learn parts; survive the inevitable hard-to-take days & **stick around for a while.**

Tips, Techniques and Tools To Master The Hunt

** Why should I pick you compared to somebody else? (*Translation*): I have many applicants; I want to avoid regretting my decision to hire you instead of any of them. I would rather eat dirt than to make an expensive, wrong decision. Tell me quickly, what makes *you best qualified*?

For your commercial, finish answering these questions in a sentence or 2, adding a how moving to **this** job makes sense to your development or the employer's needs.

Answers to these questions should be direct to what the employer's looking for and sincere in how you feel. Warning: Sometimes your preparation for answering these questions tells you something about how you really feel about your uniqueness or why the employer is uniquely special to you.

Making It Work:

Think of your four best prospective employers. Consider their point of view in the three top questions to be answered. **Now write commercial covering answers** for each of them. Note the commercials will not be identical so it will take <u>some imagination</u>. Practice the

Tips, Techniques and Tools To Master The Hunt

commercials aloud; timing each to lasts at most 20-30 seconds.

Tips, Techniques and Tools To Master The Hunt

Employer words/sights/sounds
People are creatures of habit in showing their preferences and you can see those preferences –
if you know where to look.

Hiring managers are creatures of habit, for example in sensory matters:
- In the way they talk: People tend to use expressions related to one of the five senses: They use phrases like "I SEE what you mean" or "Do you HEAR what I am saying" or "I get this FEELING…"
- They tend to emphasize that sense in their style, visual talkers more interested in how things look, feeling people more sensitive to how things "feel".
- Note the speed of their speaking delivery. Are they talking quickly, raising their voice at certain places?

Address this by trying to match the phrasing and emphasis in your own speech and appreciate the level they value on those senses (hint: visual people do not like an appearance of chaos on your desk).

They show preferences by the decisions made:
- What is on their office wall? Is it inviting, family oriented or are they meant to impress and value achievement or connections?

Tips, Techniques and Tools To Master The Hunt

- The environment – in the office and lobby is the area built for comfort, efficiency and what message is being given to the people waiting there – competence, customer service?

By knowing these things before meeting the hiring manager, you can be more prepared for that meeting.

Making It Work:

Practice these skills first with friends, clerks in stores, family – most anyone you interact with regularly. Now you may see their world from their perspective a little better.

Make your notes below of the way others see the world, or how different places are arranged. The trick again is to match your speaking style to the interests and perspective of the people you are talking with. **It takes practice** but is a lot of fun once you get used to it. So have some fun, eh?

Tips, Techniques and Tools To Master The Hunt

Failure is not a person

That phrase says it best, but it is limited. The day is long and there may be times when you feel deflated by your situation. Just remember:

"Failure" is not a person, it IS an isolated event. It is not a pattern *or a prediction* for the future or even a good description of what happened in that event – you always have the opportunity to learn from any loss or setback.

Looking at things in a larger view there are other words that may have the same temporary effect
"Disability" is not a person and neither is "unemployment", "bankruptcy", "welfare" or "poverty".
Make certain that it does not stick to you like a tattoo – it is not unless you make it one.

Making It Work:

Make a long list of words or situations used to either hurt people or to make them feel "less than" what they really are. Now make your personal list of 5 words – complete with the true definition of what that word is often associated with a certain perspective. Now include the true review of what they actually mean.

Tips, Techniques and Tools To Master The Hunt

Tips, Techniques and Tools To Master The Hunt

<u>*I know that there's a pony in there somewhere*</u>

President Ronald Reagan had a great story to tell people about his optimistic view of the world.

He said there were twin boys with ***opposite*** personalities: one always angry and negative, the other always very happy and positive. Their parents went to a psychiatrist to find a way to make the first more appreciative, the other more realistic. They were told to buy the first child a beautiful toy fire truck and the other a room full of, well, **poop**.

Upon getting the truck, the first boy shouted "Hey, I wanted a BLUE fire truck! You ***never give me what I want*** – you must hate me!" He ran away, the parents unable to speak.

The other child was then led to a room piled chest high in **poop**. The child stood thinking for a moment then jumped into the room excitedly. His parents pulled him back and asked why he did such a thing. The child said ***"With all of that poop, there must be a pony in there somewhere."***

The four lessons are
- Please do not try this experiment at home!

Tips, Techniques and Tools To Master The Hunt

- Appreciate all of the blue fire trucks or other free gifts that you receive.
- When you get a room full of stink, there is something special in there somewhere.
- When considering what you have or want, *avoid words like "always" and "never"*

Making It Work:
Keep a written record of the opportunities you come across during the day and your response. Review it later to see how you react to these opportunities.

There are other ways to detect your optimism – like putting a rubber band on your wrist then pulling it and **thwacking** yourself with it whenever you say something negative. With time you will get good on this and either train yourself to be less negative or wind up with a big pain in the wrist.

Try either or both of these for one week. ***And keep looking for that pony.***

Tips, Techniques and Tools To Master The Hunt

Tips, Techniques and Tools To Master The Hunt

Sand/glass/sand

You probably already know that **glass is made from sand**. Next chance you can, take a look at a glass made from real glass, hold it in your hand and admire it. Think for a moment that what you are holding came from ... probably sand from other parts of the world... sand for thousands of years until *for right now* it is a useful glass container that you can enjoy and use and admire.

Soon, probably way too soon, it will become broken and no longer useful as a glass. It may even eventually return to being sand again.

So much in life is like that glass... enjoying what you have until it is gone.

At the closing of an area brewery years ago, a news reporter interviewed people leaving their job for the last time (where do reporters come up interviewing people at this time is a good idea?) Along with people expressing anger, fear o, crying was one person who seemed very much at peace. He told the reporter

"Hey, I have been on this gravy train for nearly 17

Tips, Techniques and Tools To Master The Hunt

years, *now I get to see what comes next.*"

THAT is how you appreciate the sand to glass to sand in your life. Enjoy the glass knowing it will one day be sand.

Making It Work:

Make a list of the things you have in your life right now, one column for things you can see and feel and another column for things you cannot.

Now ask yourself (and make marks beside your lists):
How am I making the most of the resources I have today?
How will I cope when these gifts are no longer here?
How am I appreciating the gifts that I have today- both the gifts you can see (material, family and friends) and those you cannot (education, support)?

Tips, Techniques and Tools To Master The Hunt

The Proper Care and Feeding of References

Job hunting involves so many different things being juggled at the same time. Along with your research and rewriting of resumes, one part that is often overlooked by your competition is **caring for references.**

Often when candidates for a job are closely matched, a strong reference can carry one person over the finish line to getting the job. Where do you get references like that?

First, return to your *Oz factor*:
- Who knows of your ability to learn, understand and put things into practice? Teachers, former employers are good examples, but do not forget others who also have examples of your brains like people you have helped teach or train.
- Who knows of your abilities to get along well with others? Co-workers, sure, but do not forget about satisfied customers or people in related agencies you work with on occasion for special projects.
- Who knows of your conscientiousness and courage? Think of specific circumstances that show these traits and remember the people involved in them for

Tips, Techniques and Tools To Master The Hunt

a list of potential references.

Different examples of these factors will be important to different employers so make sure to match up the right people and examples for each job applied for.

Now contact each reference before you list them as a reference and ask them for **the privilege** of having them speak well for you to employers. After they say yes, thank them verbally and follow that up with a sign of your **appreciation** (card, gift, favor, offer of help for them).

Finally the most important parts – talk with them of examples they may bring up if/when they are called. Having these specific examples ready makes your application unique and memorable to the employer.

Finally, keep in touch with these folks because that call to them reminding them of how you **appreciate** their support may yield not only their help but also lets them know you are looking – they may have some leads for your hunt.

Keep them up to date, if they would like, with your progress as people often enjoy being part of something bigger than themselves like being part of your success story.

Making It Work:
Review the lesson and follow the steps provided:
- List your Oz factor and the people who could

Tips, Techniques and Tools To Master The Hunt

   support your claims to brains, heart and courage.
- Connect those people and the Oz factors to be presented to the employers and what they would value.
- Contact those people and ask if they would do you the favor of being a reference.
- Remind them of great points they could raise if contacted by an employer. This avoids the situation where an employer calls a reference and gets "uh… George, huh? George Valentine… oh, yeh, great guy…" and instead gets "George, great guy, let me tell you about him…"
- THANK THEM and keep in touch every so often in your hunt.

Enjoy the day, folks.

Tips, Techniques and Tools To Master The Hunt

Spirit: Making YOU More Interesting

Think of the more interesting people you know – either personally or by their reputation. Although their outward attractiveness is part of what makes them special, it is a certain part of their personality that gives them that something special.

There is **something *unchanging* in them** no matter the temporary situation that they are in. This 'extra' lifts them up when they are down, supporting their courage, warms their heart helping in their relationships with others and provides their confidence when having to learn, understand and accomplish things before them.

That something special is inside and can be strengthened by certain actions. **You** can build that something special and make yourself more interesting at the same time.

Making It Work:
- "Fake it till you make it". I am not saying to be someone you are not, but put on a temporary mask of someone with confidence when you are hurting until the pain goes away. "Tough times don't last

Tips, Techniques and Tools To Master The Hunt

but tough people do."
- Help someone. I've mentioned this earlier in the series, but it gives you a chance to be appreciated by someone who sees you as part of the solution for their needs. If you ever saw the TV show "Cheers", you remember the scene when Norm would walk in and the place would erupt with people calling "Norm!" THIS is what helping others or volunteering would do for you – gives you the "Norm!" effect.
- Learn about and begin traditions (faith, family, etc.) that can give your life a greater sense of rhythm and balance. You may be surprised.
- Read something inspirational whether a biography, quotations or short stories. Make this a habit.
- Learn something new – especially if it is something you have meant to do. It will distract your mind for a while and give you something new in your life.
- Make a finished product whether a meal, woodworking, knitting – it does not matter. It is a special feeling when you are involved in something as "unfinished" as job hunting where you are always in the process of something, to have made a finished product you are proud of.

Take a look at these ideas and select three or four most appropriate for you. And see them through.

Tips, Techniques and Tools To Master The Hunt

Employment agencies

Most job hunters have a pretty clear view of how to prepare for an employer's Oz factor and their perspective of the kind of person they want for a particular job. You apply for Job A after researching just what the employer wants in that position. You pare down and focus your resume with your skills and capabilities and ready for structured interview targeting this one job – like all of the interviews before. Then you wait a while for them to make their decision.

When you make application to an employment agency – forget all that about the other kind of interviewing.

Most employment or staffing agencies (the ones that do not specialize in a narrow part of the employment market) have no idea what kind job they will have open when you arrive or the next day or the next.

Even with those agencies that specialize in a certain field (accounting or nursing for example) or have openings at a particular field operation (such as a factory or warehouse) do not know what opening they will have to fill next.

Tips, Techniques and Tools To Master The Hunt

How does that affect you and the next interview?
Five ways.

- You should tell them everything about your skills, abilities since you will be considered for a wide range of jobs, not just one.
- Show your *energy* and availability. Be peppy, showing that you have the interest and energy for whatever comes along. Stress that you have transportation to make it to the jobsite (be honest as saying you can get there then saying "sorry, I can't" may hurt your chances for jobs in the future.
- Show **initiative and persistence**. Keep in touch with the agency with regular, polite calls about your availability and skills you have. Keep looking for their local ads indicating work available and when calling indicate you would like to be considered for them. Some interviewers may try to get past "practiced enthusiasm" of some applicants by asking some stress questions. Just relax and be yourself.
- <u>Say thank you</u>. Be memorable (in a good way) with the agency and with the specialist who interviewed you. As someone who worked in those shoes, thank you notes are rare and memorable.
- Beware the "one strike and you're out" that many agencies have – once placed get there, do your job and avoid conflicts when you can. Due to the nature of employment agencies avoid the temptation to say at a placement "hey, I won't do THAT". It

Tips, Techniques and Tools To Master The Hunt

may be your last placement with that agency.

Making It Work:
Go for it! Make application to an employment agency with either a real or practice interview. Know your Oz factor well and be ready to express several aspects of it.

Get several ads for specific jobs from employment agencies and complete blank general applications for each of them. See how different they are? See how the different the interviews and perspective of the hiring manager will be? Go ahead and keep in mind the five clues in this lesson.

Notes:

Tips, Techniques and Tools To Master The Hunt

Higher Power

When facing a task like job hunting, it's good to know you are not alone.

Whatever your beliefs, have him take a moment and **recall the great wonders of the world** we share... the sound of thunder, the miracle of birth, the smell of hot pretzels. And, hey, you are one of those wonders, too... and the world would be less 'rich' without you.

Believing that much, that little mustard seed of belief, makes the sun shine brighter and makes the darkness a *little* easier to take.

Making It Work:

Make a list of *twenty-five wonders* ... things that would make you stand back in your daily life and say 'hey, that is alright'. Maybe sunsets or a friend's laugh or an unexpected kindness given to you... its your list and your decisions.

Tips, Techniques and Tools To Master The Hunt

Now make a new list of *twenty-five more wonders*. Take time considering the wonders a gift to you or the world in general, like soft rain, holding a baby or the opportunity to sing. Maybe help out by making your own list along with them.

Thank you…

Thank you for completing the JHTK program. The tasks ahead are do-able and the tools you already have can help you build a new future. Keep these lessons and exercises close by and try going over them again in the future.

Know that you have what it takes to build that future and when the clouds gather and the cold winds blow (they always will), you will be ready.

The only weather phenomenon that happens everywhere in the world is the thunderstorm.

You can be afraid of the noise and lightning – or you can see it as a wonderful example of nature's majesty. Air that had been still and was destined for change will soon change and fresh air will come after the racket of wind and noise passes. The storm will rage no matter how you look at it,

Tips, Techniques and Tools To Master The Hunt

you might as well be prepared and enjoy it.

The job hunt is your own personal thunderstorm and now you have the opportunity to be ready for it. Good luck and look out for the Job Hunting Tool Kit for more help in the future.

www.ingramcontent.com/pod-product-compliance
Lightning Source LLC
Chambersburg PA
CBHW071758200526
45167CB00017B/415